WE PRAY WITH HER

WE PRAY WITH HER

Encouragement for All Women Who Lead

Emily Peck-McClain,
Danyelle Trexler,
Jen Tyler, J. Paige Boyer,
Shannon Sullivan

ABINGDON PRESS

NASHVILLE

WE PRAY WITH HER
ENCOURAGEMENT FOR ALL WOMEN WHO LEAD

Copyright © 2018 by Abingdon Press

All rights reserved.

Library of Congress Cataloging-in-Publication Data has been requested.
ISBN 978-1-5018-6970-9

Scripture quotations are taken from the Common English Bible, copyright 2011. Used by permission. All rights reserved.

Scripture quotations marked (NIV) are taken from the Holy Bible, New International Version®, NIV®. Copyright © 1973, 1978, 1984, 2011 by Biblica, Inc.™ Used by permission of Zondervan. All rights reserved worldwide. www.zondervan.com The "NIV" and "New International Version" are trademarks registered in the United States Patent and Trademark Office by Biblica, Inc.™

Scripture quotations marked NLT are taken from the Holy Bible, New Living Translation, copyright ©1996, 2004, 2015 by Tyndale House Foundation. Used by permission of Tyndale House Publishers, Inc., Carol Stream, Illinois 60188. All rights reserved.

Scripture quotations marked NRSV are taken from the New Revised Standard Version Bible, copyright © 1989 National Council of the Churches of Christ in the United States of America. Used by permission. All rights reserved worldwide. http://nrsvbibles.org/.

18 19 20 21 22 23 24 25 26—10 9 8 7 6 5 4 3 2 1
MANUFACTURED IN THE UNITED STATES OF AMERICA

Contents

COURAGE

RESISTANCE

PERSISTENCE

Foreword

W*e Pray With Her.* This phrase is powerful, each word shimmering with significance.

We is our reality. Human beings are made to be together. We're made through relationship for relationship—relationship with other people, with creation, and with God. In companionship and community we come to know ourselves and what it means to be human—its beauty and its pain. Christian scripture—and wisdom from across cultures—teaches that we are interconnected like the parts of one human body. As Dr. Martin Luther King Jr. wrote in his letter from the Birmingham jail, "We are caught in an inescapable network of mutuality." *We* are in this thing together.

To *pray* is to consciously acknowledge God's presence and power in the midst of all life's circumstances. The words "thoughts and prayers" are overused and sometimes abused in the public square and, as a result, may seem empty for some. But for anyone who has been in a place of pain, grief, stress, or challenge and had a community truly holding you in prayer, you know that the prayers and loving thoughts of others have a mysterious way of buoying your life through the storm. For anyone who has hit rock bottom and discovered that Spirit was there to gather you up in her arms, you know that prayer is not empty, but full of the love and mercy of a gracious God. Anyone who regularly prays—through the myriad forms that may take—will understand that through prayer God moves our heart, mind, and will; prayer leads us into lives of greater awareness, integrity, freedom, purpose, and action.

With is a joining word, a relational word, an assurance that you are not alone, that someone has your back, that you are remembered, that the despair or joy or fear you're experiencing or that space between a rock and hard place in which you find yourself is something others know intimately. The heart of the gospel is the appearance in flesh of *Emmanuel*, God with us. It is deeply human to yearn to be with someone who loves you. And the life of Jesus reveals that it is also profoundly human to offer yourself—to be with others—in solidarity and friendship so that they might know the love of God in flesh.

And what of *her*? What about *her*? Meditate on that word for even a moment and it conjures women at every age and stage of life, women in every place and land, women in power and those who feel powerless, women bleeding from giving birth and women bleeding because they are yet again not pregnant. *Her* life is the life of both presidents and prostitutes, of soccer moms and secretaries of state, of day laborers, nail technicians, CEOs, ranch hands, artists, pastors, poets, cooks, teachers, scientists, and on it goes. What about her? She is—as she has always been—a powerful force, a source of strength and creativity and connection, a lover and a fighter, a doer and a dreamer. She may not always remember her worth or her capacity, but that doesn't diminish the inevitable truth of her significance. *Her...* Yes. She is a beloved child of God.

In the following pages you will discover yourself walking with her—particularly as she navigates the earlier life stages of the journey. As you reflect on the devotions and pray the prayers in this book, you take your place among a community of women who—with extraordinary wisdom and insight—offer their lives to you, inviting you to pray with them, to join them in the wondrous mess and gift that is life with one another and with God. *We pray with her.* And she prays with us. And God is with us on the way. Thanks be to God.

Ginger E. Gaines-Cirelli
Senior Pastor, Foundry UMC

Call

Call is that deep sense of knowing that God is beckoning you in a way of being, a kind of work, and a new way of making a difference in the world.

When we talk about *calling*, we affirm the idea that there are things in our lives and work that speak into the deep places of our souls. These calls are the places where our gifts take root and blossom within the soil of deep purpose. For some, calling is perennial, blooming over and over again in the springs of our lives. For others, calls are more akin to annuals or biannuals and are replanted over different seasons.

We often shortchange ourselves, and others, when we talk about calling as being only for those serving in ministry. While that is the lens and the context for many of our writers, God calls everyone: those who lead companies, communities, nonprofits, families, and churches. Calls, too, are about both the things that earn us money and the things that bring us joy—and they aren't always the same thing.

Cultivating our calls is rarely straightforward or simple. Even when we are filled with assurance, we may hit bumps along the way. The devotions and prayers that follow remind us we aren't alone when we find ourselves a little unsure or disheartened. Women called to lead, whether in homes, churches, business, or politics, take this path together.

We are not alone, for the land has been tilled, and God meets us along the way, watering the seeds planted deep in our souls. God is with us, pursuing us and encouraging us during every season.

Don't be intimidated by successful makers; be inspired by them.[1]

—*Jen Hatmaker*

Sometimes we hear the still small voice inside calling us to create, and we shush it, ignore it, or intentionally push it away. The voice whispers to us to make a piece of art, bring a vision to reality, write the story that's longing to get out, or try something new in our work.

With the still, small voice, God is trying to do a new thing in and through us, but we push it away thinking, *This has already been done before* or *Someone else could do this so much better than I could.*

We may consider ourselves too amateur, too inexperienced, too uneducated, or too poorly connected to bring our creations into the world. We may wonder why anyone would look at, use, or be inspired by things coming out of our imaginations. We may be afraid that our attempts will fail, that we will be laughed at or ignored, that someone else could have done it better.

We are each created in the image of a creative God, a God with such wild imagination that our lives are full of sunsets and narwhals and brussels sprouts and twenty-eight thousand species of orchids and mountains and rivers and ornery house cats. Part of growing in God's likeness is letting that still, small voice out of its cage and doing its bidding. Part of our role as human beings, made in God's image, is to create, whether we are amateurs or professionals, first-time creators or polished experts. Instead of looking around and saying, "No, I'm not really good enough to create this," we offer our unique gifts to God and the world around us. Instead of being intimidated by those who have found worldly success in whatever realm we are called to enter, God beckons us to let our imaginations lead where they may and bring our creations to life.

Do not be intimidated by those who have come before you or those who will come after you, dear sister. Don't let fear stop you. Don't sell yourself short because you're not a "professional" or an "expert." Take courage from the God who created you and me and all we can see—everything useful or beautiful or strange—and let that voice speak until your extraordinary creations have been born. You never know who you will inspire with your courage, whose voice will speak louder because of yours.

Prayer: O God, help me never silence my own inner voice because I am afraid or intimidated by others. Give me the courage to create whatever you have put into my heart, for your glory. Amen.

Rev. Elizabeth Ingram Schindler

"Ah, LORD God," I said, "I don't know how to speak
    because I'm only a child."
The LORD responded,
    "Don't say, 'I'm only a child.'
        Where I send you, you must go;
        what I tell you, you must say.
Don't be afraid of them,
    because I'm with you to rescue you,"
        declares the LORD.

—Jeremiah 1:6-8

Following God's call is never an easy thing. Following God with our whole lives often means being uncomfortable or challenged. In the midst of challenges, it can be easy to feel unprepared and unequipped to go where God is sending us and to do what God is asking of us. Jeremiah felt this when God called him to be a prophet. He immediately responded by saying that he was too young and not a good speaker.

I wish I could say that my response to God's call to be a pastor was different than Jeremiah's, more like Mary of Nazareth's agreeing to bear the Christ child than the argument we see from so many of the other prophets. I was seventeen and couldn't stand in front of others and talk without my voice and hands shaking from being so nervous. I felt unprepared and unequipped. There was no way I could be a pastor speaking in front of others, teaching, and being a leader!

But even when God calls us to something we don't think we can do or makes us afraid, God promises to be with us, just like with Jeremiah. God doesn't abandon us but rather journeys with us through the unknown, and through the learning and the growing we must do. When we take seriously the call God has placed upon lives, when we go where God sends us, and when we open ourselves up to the presence of God with us and within us, we can experience a peace that only comes from God. A peace that washes over us and fills us with joy and lets us know that we are a part of God's work in the world.

Prayer: "Ah, Lord God," sometimes I don't want to do what you have called me to do. Sometimes I'm afraid, I doubt my abilities, or I just don't want to do it because it will be hard work. Keep calling out to me, keep pushing me, and open my heart to listening and doing your work in the world. Thank you for promising to be with me even when I doubt or worry. Amen.

Rev. Jessica Lauer Baldyga

"Be still, and know that I am God! I am exalted among the nations, I am exalted in the earth." The LORD *of hosts is with us; the God of Jacob is our refuge.*

—*Psalm 46:10-11 NRSV*

I am an independent, go-getter who tends to move at full speed. Perhaps you are too. That is what it takes to be a woman in leadership. Better than average is not enough. Exceptional may still fall short. When it comes to leading people who do not want a woman (especially a young woman, especially a single one) leading them, there may be nothing I can do right. When I found myself in that hopelessly frustrating place of rejection, I gave up. I gave up trying to rely only on my expertise and my people skills. I gave up trying to be above reproach. I gave up trying to meet other people's expectations. Instead, I sought to lead from a place of stillness and knowledge that God is God.

Paired with prayer and discernment, learning to "be still and know" that he is God has shown me how to recognize the presence of I Am within me. The psalmist's words take me to a place of humility where I recognize that my call is always to live and lead in such a way that God is exalted.

When the powers that be reject my leadership, I am still called to lead. When the people I lead are angry that I ask them to change, I am just getting started. When the old guard ignores my authority, I am willing to take them on. When I am coming from a place of stillness, grounded in the faith that I Am dwells within me, I am powerful and persistent. I Am does not back down in the face of adversity, nor will I. And when leading boldly wears me down, I am not alone—and neither are you. "The Lord of hosts is with us; the God of Jacob is our refuge."

Prayer: God, you have called me to lead, but I call upon you to lead through me. When there is turmoil within or around me, be still with me. When I am too beaten down to go on, be my refuge. When there is more work to be done, return to the fray with me as I seek to show the world I Am within me. Amen.

Rev. Karen Hernandez

∽ A Prayer for Discernment ∽

God of hope, shine light in my life.

I am seeking and searching, and I am looking for guidance.

I pray that you will give me ears to hear, eyes to see, and a heart open to possibilities.

Let me hear your truth in the voices of the wise people in my life.

Let me know your truth in my own wisdom.

Keep me from rushing at easy answers, God.

Help me have patience to wait, to watch, to sit

long enough to listen and let the answers unfold before me.

Help me trust my own knowing when the answer makes itself known.

Be with me in the waiting and watching, God. Be with me.

Amen.

Rev. Anjie Peek Woodworth

∽ A Prayer Before an Important Meeting ∽

Creator God, be with everyone who will gather for this meeting. Lead us and guide us. Help us hear the wisdom of one another. In the midst of it all, help me stay centered in you. It is in you that I find my strength and my worth. Be with me as I go into this meeting. Give me wisdom and courage, patience and ears to hear, and guide my words and actions. I root myself in your love, first and always. May it be so. Amen.

Rev. Anjie Peek Woodworth

O how careful ought we to be, lest through our by-laws of church government and church discipline, we bring into disrepute even the word of life.[2]

—*Jarena Lee*

I have always known I wanted to be a mom. I don't even know when I first realized it, but I have always known it deep in my bones. I have three kids who are a constant source of joy and busyness and humility. I am also an ordained minister and a seminary professor. I know that these are all my call, my vocation. I know this because I am passionately alive when I am fulfilling my calls to motherhood, ministry, and teaching.

I didn't meet an ordained woman until the summer before seminary. I still don't know how I thought I could even be a pastor, except I know the Spirit must have called it forth in my imagination. But here's the thing: I have been told I shouldn't preach because I am a woman. I have been told that since I am a mother, that is my only call and I am betraying my children and my God by working at all.

It is sometimes impossible to hear God's gentle and consistent Spirit over the constant din of other people telling us what we should be doing with our time and energy. The hardest voices to ignore are the voices from within the church.

Jarena Lee, an African American preacher in the 1800s, faced many people within the church telling her that what she knew to be from God was wrong. She questioned the call herself and asked God about it repeatedly, but in the end, it was clear and became clear to others too. She became the first woman authorized by the African Methodist Episcopal Church to preach.

Women who are called to both motherhood and work outside the home will be questioned, sometimes combatively. We will face people who don't understand or respect the call we know is from God.

The church should not be part of the problem. The church should help us discern our call and support us when it inevitably becomes difficult to juggle more than one call faithfully.

Jarena Lee knew that betraying a call from God, even when the church was the one telling her to, would bring "into disrepute even the word of life." May she help us follow in her footsteps.

Prayer: God who knows my gifts and limitations better than I do, lead me to live a life that honors your word of life. Clear away the doubts that come from listening to people who don't understand your call for me. Amen.

Rev. Dr. Emily A. Peck-McClain

The doorframe shook at the sound of their shouting, and the
house was filled with smoke. I said, "Mourn for me; I'm ruined!
I'm a {person} with unclean lips, and I live among a people with
unclean lips. Yet I've seen the king, the Lord of heavenly forces!"

—Isaiah 6:4-5

As women, often the hardest thing for us isn't hearing our call—it's believing it. *How can I possibly be called? I'm not smart enough, strong enough, or good enough*, we think. It is comforting to know that even the Hebrew prophet Isaiah had those thoughts. Just as God was asking Isaiah to be God's spokesperson to Israel, Isaiah was protesting, "But I'm a person of unclean lips! Surely you can find someone better to do this job." But God doesn't choose someone else. God sends Isaiah.

Likewise, we often hear a call to do important work in our world, but we feel inadequate. *If I just had a few more skills*, we think. *If I just knew a bit more, had a bit more experience, or had more time to prepare, then I would be ready*. Even once we've followed a call, we can still feel like we don't measure up. These feelings affect everyone. Psychologists call this "Imposter Syndrome," the feeling that at any time someone will discover that we're a fake and don't really deserve to be where we are.

We describe this feeling in another way as "waiting for the other shoe to drop," waiting for something bad to happen, waiting for someone to find us out. But as writer Anne Lamott once quipped, "I think God only has one shoe."[3] The God of love isn't going to deceive us.

What's important is that Isaiah doesn't listen to that gut reaction that says he's not good enough. Isaiah listens to God's voice instead. When God asks who will go to the people, Isaiah says, "I'm here; send me." God didn't make a mistake in calling Isaiah. God needed exactly what Isaiah had to offer—good, bad, or otherwise.

The God who created us needs exactly what we have to offer, too. God doesn't make mistakes when calling us, even if we sometimes feel unworthy. God has called you, not in spite of who you are, but because of who you are.

Prayer: Loving God, you create us and are the first to speak our names. You call us to important work in your world. Help us to listen to your voice, especially when other voices tell us we're unworthy. Help us to continue to answer your call. In the name of Jesus we pray. Amen.

Rev. Monica D. Beacham

*{Martha} had a sister named Mary, who sat at the Lord's feet
and listened to his message. By contrast, Martha was preoccupied
with getting everything ready for their meal. So Martha came to
him and said, "Lord, don't you care that my sister has left me to
prepare the table all by myself? Tell her to help me."*

—Luke 10:39-40

I've struggled with this scene from Luke, where Jesus is at Martha's home for dinner. I'm uncomfortable with the way Mary and Martha are seemingly pitted against each other, and how Jesus dismisses Martha's service in favor of Mary's sitting and listening to him. It seems to me that both roles are valuable. And if Martha had stopped working, no one would have eaten dinner that night.

I recently read a thoughtful essay on this familiar passage that blew it open in a whole new way. Mary A. Hanson wrote, "I do not think that there is even evidence that Mary is in the house that day. . . . Mary is not there. She is gone! [Martha's] stress is due to worry about her sister being . . . on the road with Jesus in ministry."[4] My first response was shock. I quickly turned back to the scripture to double check—Mary was present at this meal, right?

But in fact, rereading the passage anew through the lens offered by Hanson, I could see a whole new possibility. Martha welcomes Jesus to dinner because she is the one who is still at home. But the language used to describe Mary suggests someone who is a disciple of a teacher taking the characteristic posture of sitting at the teacher's feet. She's a disciple, not just in this fixed setting, but as a life path. The part Mary has chosen is the part of discipleship. Martha hasn't chosen that path, at least not yet. By answering the call to follow Jesus, Mary accepts a perilous path for a woman in the first century. Martha isn't ready, however, and that's OK. But Jesus won't allow Martha to hinder Mary's bold journey of faith by making her conform to the social norms of the day. Mary doesn't have to fit the status quo to follow Jesus.

God is continually calling us, asking us for a bold response, seeking our risk-taking discipleship. It's always easier to remain in our predetermined, comfortable, status-quo safe places than to hit the road with Jesus; but only in following him can we truly find the better part. May we be bold answering the call, again and again.

Prayer: Holy God, help me choose the better part and boldly answer your call. Amen.

Rev. Dr. Elizabeth Quick

A Prayer for an Important Interview

May I trust you, O God, the source of all I am, all I have, and all I have done.

May I trust the gift within me that comes from you.

May I believe you have called me to reflect your light the way a diamond reflects the sun.

May I believe I am part of your ongoing creating.

May I know whatever happens, your love is my origin.

May I know whatever form my life's work takes, love is my purpose.

May I speak and listen, learn and hope, wait and move.

May I live with this awareness deep in my bones, my brain, my heart.

Amen.

Rev. Alison VanBuskirk Philip

A Prayer for Dropping a Baby Off at Day Care for the First Time

Mothering God, hold me close today as I take this step as a working mother.

Be in the tears that I cry as I grieve the loss of time with my baby. Comfort me, hold me close, and whisper that my baby knows I love them.

Be in the butterflies in my stomach as I try to remember diapers and wipes, bottles and burp cloths. Be in the nervousness of trying to adjust to a new schedule and divide my time, energy, and attention in new ways.

Be in the deep breaths I take as I prepare to leave my child in the care of someone else.

Be in the release as I seek to let go of guilt, anxiety, and fear.

Be in my hopes as I consider the work that I am called to do. I hope my time is well spent. I hope to reconnect with colleagues and the normalcy of my routine at work. I hope my work is meaningful. I hope my time at work helps me to be all the more grateful for the time I will spend with my child when the workday ends.

You are with me in the work I do, and you are with those who will care for my child. Give me peace, knowing that my little one will be well taken care of while I attend to other things. Amen.

Rev. Dr. Emily A. Peck-McClain

Our truest calling is where our talents and burdens collide. We must find those God-gifts that make us uniquely us, and then pair them with a burden that those gifts fit like a key.[5]

—*Rebekah Lyons*

I used to think of my calling to ministry as a static, one-time event that happened when I was seventeen years old, the night I heard God's voice asking me to "feed the sheep." After some initial doubts, I pursued that calling single-mindedly. By twenty-four, I was serving my first congregation as a United Methodist pastor. My experiences there served as a confirmation of my calling. I thought I had arrived.

Over the next few years, I came to recognize calling as a continual process rather than a static event. I found my calling evolving based on my gifts, passions, and settings. I ministered in ways I had never previously considered: coaching churches through transformation and mentoring new candidates and clergy. Rebekah Lyons reminds us that our talents are "God-gifts," which make us unique in our response. But, I had not yet found the place where my God-given gifts and my burdens actually collided. That did not come until I emerged from a dark period in my midthirties during which both of my parents died. For almost two years, I had made weekly trips home to help manage their care, while still juggling being a wife, mother, and pastor.

What emerged from that period was a deep burden for clergy who are navigating ministry while experiencing grief, illness, and other stressful personal circumstances. This completely reshaped the focus of my mentoring, which became concentrated on foundations of self-care and spiritual development to sustain pastors for the long haul of ministry and to resource them for times of crisis. God redeemed one of the worst seasons of my life by using it to help others through mentoring. I would never have envisioned this at seventeen, yet it's where my burdens meet my gifts like a key.

In difficult seasons it is easy to get bogged down in life and work and lose time for self-reflection. Whatever season of life or vocation you are in right now, I encourage you to take some time to ponder your calling. Perhaps your unique "God-gifts" and the deep heart burdens you carry for people and the world already collide. But if they do not, how might you live deeper and more joyfully into your calling by aligning those two?

Prayer: Gracious God, I'm grateful for the unique ways you've shaped me and called me. May I find that place where my unique God-gifts collide with my burdens for the world and live your good news with my whole being. Amen.

Rev. Deborah Allen

As they were watching, he was lifted up and a cloud took him out of their sight. While he was going away and as they were staring toward heaven, suddenly two men in white robes stood next to them. They said, "Galileans, why are you standing here, looking toward heaven?"

—Acts 1:9b-12a

Have you had those moments where you find yourself startled, because you've been staring off into the distance and every bit of your focus is trained toward something and then suddenly, someone calls your name? You snap out of it and realize that, while your eyes and mind were trained elsewhere, the world was still moving by all around you.

At the moment of the Ascension, the disciples were left to fend for themselves. I wholly resonate with this group who decided to plant their feet firmly in the ground, looking up to where they last saw their leader—don't you? It takes so much effort and ingenuity to create your own way. But then these two men come along and call to them.

"Why are you standing here, looking toward heaven?" The part of call I struggle with the most is the moving—the doing, the responding. The piece that forces you to do more than say yes and to get to work! But there is so much wrapped up in this move from affirmation to action. It challenges our comfort, because what lies ahead is unknown. We question our capacity to perform, or whether or not we will fit in. And seriously: doing the new, big, important thing—that just takes energy, and who among us has that to spare?

Just about anything in our lives can serve the role of these two mystery men. People or places that help us to snap out of it and bring our attention to a different plane. A jarring headline that serves as a reminder of the suffering around the world. The young mom struggling to manage two kids and a shopping cart at the grocery store. The sudden scent of fresh flowers as spring awakens on the earth. That person standing on the street corner asking for help. Any of these situations might serve the purpose these two men after the Ascension did. They become someone asking, "Why are you straining your neck, staring up into the sky? God is asking you to be present, look out, look ahead, and get moving. Get involved."

Prayer: Dear God, keep me alert to the people and situations calling me forward. May I find within myself the bravery to be called forth, so that I may partner with you in the work to be done in the world. Amen.

Rev. Mara Bailey

Then I heard the voice of the Lord saying, "Whom shall I send, and who will go for us?" And I said, "Here am I; send me!"

—Isaiah 6:8 NRSV

Sometimes I am envious of Isaiah and the other prophets, not because of what they are called to (for most of them, it is a pretty tough gig), but because their call is clear. Isaiah has a vision of the Lord seated on the throne. Although it might have been fairly one-sided, they have a conversation. Like it or not, Isaiah knew what God was calling him to do.

I cannot count the times in my life that I have agonized over a decision when I was unclear about my calling. The times I have fallen on my knees and begged, "Just tell me what to do and I'll do it." Yet, as I look back on those times, often God was being clearer than I realized. However, I was not in the correct posture to listen.

If you read in the earlier verses of chapter 6, Isaiah appears humbled and overwhelmed. Yet, we see time and time again that God is especially partial to the lost and broken, and God loves to call the lost and broken to be part of God's work. In the presence of God, Isaiah recognizes his own brokenness and repents. In response, a seraph flies to Isaiah and places a hot coal on his lips to blot out his sin and remove his guilt. Now Isaiah is ready. When God calls out, "Whom shall I send, and who will go for us?" I imagine Isaiah cautiously yet confidently responding, "Here am I; send me!"

Too often I find myself lost and overwhelmed by my brokenness and am unable to hear God's call. I wallow in my faults rather than letting my guilt be removed. Sometimes I do not like the call I think I hear, so I use my unworthiness as an excuse. God usually manages to get past my resistance, and once I am able to push aside my insecurities and fear, I find myself both humbled and empowered as I cautiously yet confidently respond, "Here I am; send me!"

God is calling you. What is keeping you from saying yes?

Prayer: God of grace, remove any barriers that keep me from hearing your call on my life and strengthen me to respond, "Send me." Amen.

Rev. Laura-Allen Kerlin

A Prayer of Gratitude for When a Pregnancy Test Is Positive

Creator of us all, in this moment of emotion, I turn to you.

What a gift it is to be able to cradle life in my body, to witness its slow and mysterious shaping within. And yet, at the same time, what uncertainty there is as I think of the weeks and months and years ahead.

You are the Creator; I am a vessel. Whatever happens, you hold me and this little life within. Hold me closely and tenderly, as I hold this baby. Carry me in grace as I carry this baby. I ask this in the name of Jesus, whose origin in this world mirrors what is happening in my body right now. Amen.

Rev. Alison VanBuskirk Philip

A Prayer for When Someone Asks, Again, Why You Don't Have Children

Loving and faithful God, help me remember that my worth does not come from my womb and that my salvation is in Christ and not childbirth. In those times when others question or criticize, may I find my rest in your loving embrace. I am your beloved child and my value comes from you, and from you alone. May I come to the joy of new life by partnering in your creative work in the world. Amen.

Rev. J. Paige Boyer

*Finally these women grasp the reason why they are able to keep
dancing in the dark, to keep attending to their call to ministry.
They can trust that they are in the midst of a dark transition
into a more inclusive and mature church.*[6]

—*Joann Wolski Conn*

Whenever I can't find the words to say, I dance. When my pain is too much to bear and sighs are too deep for words, I dance. When my praise is ecstatic and I am at a loss for words, I dance.

Our lives are a dance with God. We take a step, and God responds. God calls us forward and we go. There are days when my colleagues and I talk about throwing in the towel because we are tired of wading through the sexism and ageism and other "isms" we face as we live out our callings. But our divine dance partner calls us forward and we stay in the dance. We know that in this great dance—no matter how difficult the steps—we are changing lives and touching hearts and being the hands and feet of Christ.

Women who came before us and who will come after us are dancing with God. Each and every step, both ours and God's, affects the next. I hope that each generation of women invites the next into the movement, just like the generations that came before invited them. Part of our dance is that when we are invited in, others welcome us. Part of our dance is welcoming others into the dance too.

Prayer: Loving God, you call me to go places where it is difficult to go—inside of myself and out in the world. Light the way for me so that I may continue to dance with you, in places both light and dark. Shine your light so that I may believe in miracles. Amen.

Rev. Julia Singleton

Whoever is faithful with little is also faithful with much.

—Luke 16:10a

Sometimes a pressure creeps into my heart to do great things—to stand up for justice in big ways, to say or write something moving and impactful, to help make noticeable, quantifiable changes in my community.

Of course these things are important and needed. But more often what God asks me to do is to persist in doing small things with great love. Sometimes my call is to help my daughter treat a classmate with kindness. Sometimes it is to sit with someone hurting even though it seems to make no difference. Sometimes it is to initiate a hard but important conversation. Sometimes it is to offer quiet grace to someone undeserving.

It is small acts like these that knit the fabric of society together when it seems to be coming apart. It is small acts like these that are the cobblestones that eventually create a hope-filled road forward into the future.

While leadership can mean orchestrating big things, on a day-to-day basis it often involves faithful attention to small details. It involves being aware of our particular moment in time and our particular place in our community. And then it involves navigating our way through those things with as much love as we can muster.

Our faithfulness in small things lays the groundwork for any big things that God might be preparing. Our attention to small things is a model for those we lead to be attentive in their small things. Our humility in small things points to the path taught by Jesus, whose grace is sufficient for us, who helps us in our weakness, and who is the source of the great love that the world needs more than anything else.

So from time to time I take an inventory of my life: What are the seemingly insignificant things requiring my attention? How can I bring as much love as I can muster into these things? Where is God's presence in them?

Prayer: God of all things great and small, draw my attention to what you ask me to do with great love. Open my heart to love deeply and fully as a way of reflecting your light in the relationships and tasks you have given me. Help me lead in faith that you are the author of love that binds together things small and things great. Amen.

Rev. Alison VanBuskirk Philip

But now, says the LORD—the one who created you, Jacob, the one who formed you, Israel: Don't fear, for I have redeemed you; I have called you by name; you are mine.

—*Isaiah 43:1*

There have been more than a few times in my life when I have not felt up to the task before me. Most of us have experienced feelings of insecurity, uncertainty, and self-doubt. We have questioned our abilities: Am I brave enough, am I strong enough, am I talented enough? We may see ourselves as unable or unworthy to fulfill God's call in our lives. We have reasons and excuses for why we are not the right person for the job. We could make endless lists of our inadequacies and shortcomings, our mistakes and sins, our lack of abilities or skills. We may feel like we don't have what it takes to do anything for God. Our fears and doubts keep us from responding to God's call.

But in these moments, we can trust in God's promises. When Israel wondered how they could be the people of God after all their mistakes and while in exile, the prophet Isaiah reminded them that they were created and formed by God and that God called them by name, giving them an identity and a purpose. We, too, have been created and formed by God and called to be God's people, working alongside God in the world.

The good news of God's love and grace is that God calls us not because of who we are but because of who God is. God, the Creator, Redeemer, and Sustainer, looks at you and me and all of us and says, "I have called you by name; you are mine." We belong to God, and God loves us fiercely. We are already enough for God, and God makes us enough for the call we have received.

Prayer: Gracious God, who has created and called me, speak to me in my times of doubt and fear and remind me that I belong to you. Amen.

Rev. Jodie Ihfe

⌒ **A Prayer at the Time of Adoption** ⌒

Parent of us all, you have brought us together to form a new family, rooted in love. Help me love and truly know this child, all of their dreams and hopes, all of their joys and fears. Help me be the loving parent you have called me to be.

I lift up to you the brokenness that led to this adoption and I pray that you will continue to redeem and heal it, that you will use me as a healing agent in this child's life. I pray that you will fill our lives with love and compassion that we might share it with our community.

Be with this child, God, each and every day. Be there when I can't be. More than anything, please let this child know they are loved beyond measure. Always.

I lift my child up to you today and every day. Amen.

Rev. Anjie Peek Woodworth

*Total surrender to God must come in small details as it comes in
big details. It's nothing but a single word: Yes.*[7]

—*Mother Teresa*

During my first week of graduate school, thoughts of doubt filled my
head. "What have I done?" "Am I really called to do this?" I had grad-
uated from college a few months before and I'd had a fun summer working
as a youth director, but suddenly I felt like I had been thrown into the fire.
I saw stacks of textbooks, a plethora of papers to write, and preparation for a
first day of an internship for which I was a student chaplain at a local hospital.

On Thursday afternoon, I went home and cried. My mind was going
a million miles an hour. Questions were flooding my head. My heart was
raw. How could I faithfully do my internship when I was having a spiritual
crisis? I felt alone, and my first reaction was not to turn to God in prayer or
Scripture. In fact, what I did was get ice cream, and I enjoyed every bite. It
was delicious. However, after I got home, I realized that ice cream wasn't
what I really needed; it was time to turn to God.

I opened my Bible, determined to find stories about people who ignored
their callings. That way, I could choose my own direction, whether it was
my calling from God or not. Instead of finding the stories I wanted, I found
that one's calling included doubts, fears, confusion, and heartache. Maybe I
was in the right place after all. In every story, God was present. God called
the biblical characters by name. God called me by name too.

At the same time, I had also been reading a book by Mother Teresa, and
it helped me understand something else about calling. I learned that it is
about saying YES to God! Yes, to journey into the unknown. Yes, to going
into fear. Yes, to knowing that God is journeying with us.

What I found through that journey is that we are all called by God. It
will not always be easy or clear. It will be hard work. And we still have to
say yes. Yes, to God.

Prayer: Creator God, you created me and called me child. You call me by name. Even when I question. Even when I doubt. Thank you for calling me. Thank you for being here with me in my doubt and questioning. Amen.

Rev. Ashley Fitzpatrick Jenkins

LORD, you have examined me.

    You know me.

You know when I sit down and when I stand up.

    Even from far away, you comprehend my plans.

You study my traveling and resting.

    You are thoroughly familiar with all my ways.

There isn't a word on my tongue, LORD,

    that you don't already know completely.

                    —Psalm 139:1-4

Sitting in my mother's home office, I said: "But I don't think I can sit at someone's bedside while they take their last breath.

Those were the first words I said when I decided I couldn't do the work I felt God nudging me toward.

I moved on quickly, entering college to study education and then communications. In communications, I found the perfect place to use my gifts, talents, and passions. I was called to this work. I spent my time looking at the big picture, offering strategic visions, telling stories, and building relationships.

I took a job as a communicator for a local hospice, telling stories of those in their final days, of those very bedsides I wanted to avoid. In the midst of that work, I felt a new calling, and, as it turned out, an old nudging.

Leaving one calling for another was not an easy decision. Like most hard things, however, this was worth it.

As I trained for this new vocation, I was faced with the very reality I feared as I sat with my mother after she had a massive stroke. Late in the night, I kept watch, holding her hand as she took her last breath. As it turned out, my mom taught me that I can sit at the bedside of someone dying. In fact, sometimes that's exactly the right place for me to be.

When God calls us, it is not to the easiest and most comfortable things.

God's call changes us. God's call changes with time. We never know when God will nudge us to the next place or new thing, yet we can remain alert, listening for small voices, gentle nudges, or big pushes to live a new calling.

Prayer: Creating, calling God, help keep my ears open and eyes peeled for the ways you are moving in the midst of work. May I always be in tune to your guidance and follow where you lead. Amen.

Rev. J. Paige Boyer

Mary Magdalene left and announced to the disciples, "I've seen the Lord." Then she told them what he said to her.

—*John 20:18*

He vehemently flung his arms and words as he told me I couldn't be a pastor. My mind began to whirl at his use of Scripture. I had read those words before but had never given them much thought. Again and again, he told me that women can't lead men and that women can't speak. He told me that it is not my place, and yet, I knew God had spoken my name. God had called me forth, but I'd never been challenged in this way. I had never needed a good argument before.

I felt the Holy Spirit speak loudly in response: Mary. Mary Magdalene.

She was the first to preach Christ resurrected. "I have seen the Lord," she said to her friends, the unbelieving disciples. "I have seen the Lord." It's so simple. There is so much behind those words. That man wasn't convinced, but it didn't matter. That day changed me for good. Mary's simple statement of Christ Resurrected will always give me a voice.

The church didn't want Mary Magdalene around and yet couldn't erase her from history. Mary saw the Lord. She spent her lifetime speaking Christ's name to all who would hear, even to the halls of power.

The calling of Mary Magdalene is important. God chose her to speak in spite of her fear. As God chose Mary Magdalene, God has also chosen us. For we, too, have seen the Lord. God has spoken our names and called us forth to proclaim that truth. We speak alongside Mary that Christ is indeed resurrected.

Prayer: God of the Resurrection, help me hear your voice that I may tell the world how to seek your face. In Christ. Amen.

Rev. Sara McManus

We appealed to you, encouraged you, and pleaded with you to live lives worthy of the God who is calling you into his own kingdom and glory.

—1 Thessalonians 2:12

I've always tried to live a life worthy of God. I grew up in the church, actively participating in the congregation throughout my youth and young adulthood. Growing up, I understood living a good life, one worthy of God, in terms of "do nots." Do not listen to that music, do not watch those movies, do not say those words, do not hang out with them, do not. . . . As my faith matured, the "do nots" transformed into "dos." Do seek peace, do love the outcast, do feed the hungry and clothe the naked, do pray for one another, do speak against injustice . . .

The apostle Paul encourages the whole congregation at Thessalonica to lead lives worthy of God. It's the fellowship of believers supporting one another that will make them most successful. By having others walking alongside you, following the list of "dos" with you, seeking after God's ways rather than the ways of the world, then you are most successful. So, we must encourage one another to persevere as we lead lives worthy of God's call.

Our calls may look very different. Some of us are stay-at-home moms, others are doctors and attorneys, some are bus drivers, food servers, CEOs, or teachers. Some of us work in an office but find our call in going on mission trips or teaching yoga. But we are all women striving to lead lives worthy of God. By supporting and encouraging one another along the way, we have a better chance of faithfully serving God than if we try to serve alone.

Just as Paul encouraged the church in Thessalonica, we as Christian women must inspire one another—walk side by side—to lead lives worthy of God.

Prayer: Holy God, who knows all and calls me by name, help me remember that no matter my profession, my family situation, my age, or my gender, my calling is the same as all Christians: to seek after your ways. Guide me as I follow your calling: to live a life worthy of you. Amen.

Rev. Katrina Paxson

~ A Prayer for When the ~ Caregiver Needs Care

Merciful God, so often I care for others, but I now find myself having to rely on others to care for me. I feel like such a burden, though in reality I know that I need help. Help me reach out. Soften my heart to accept this support and to welcome it with a gladness and thanksgiving. I praise you for this gift and give thanks for my many blessings. Watch over me, dear Lord, and may this be a time of rest and of healing. Amen.

Rev. Jennifer Zeigler Medley

~ A Prayer When Returning ~ from Vacation

Thank you, God, for this time I have had away. It was amazing to set aside the pressures and stressors of work. Thank you for the chance to relax, to sleep in, to have new adventures, and to just be me.

I have felt your blessings with me every step of the way. I am thankful for the privilege to go on vacation.

As I step back into the real world, help me take this mind-set with me back to work. Help me find peace in chaos, joy in trouble, and rest in exhaustion. May I now bring fresh ideas and new life into my work. Above all, I pray this work is done to your glory, just as my rest is to your glory. In Christ's name. Amen.

Rev. Heather Dorr

Curiosity only ever asks one simple question: "Is there anything you're interested in?" . . . if you can pause and identify even one tiny speck of interest in something, then curiosity will ask you to turn your head a quarter of an inch and look at the thing a wee bit closer.[8]

—*Elizabeth Gilbert*

This quotation takes me back to a discernment group I was a part of in college. Like most college-aged students, we were feeling pressured to decide what we wanted to do for the rest of our lives. We were feeling lost and longing for our own proverbial burning bushes that would tell us exactly what we should do.

I was once on retreat with this group of peers talking about our shared desire to do this well. In an effort to bring forth clarity, our facilitator asked us a question that ties closely to the words Gilbert offers us. "What should our vocation be?" our facilitator asked. "It should be doing the one thing you can't imagine not doing."

At first, I had to really think about this. But before long, I realized that if there is one thing in my life I can't imagine not doing, it would be to be involved at a church. I couldn't imagine a life in which the church was not a part of my weekly, if not daily, life. I had no idea what shape that would take, but it did invite me to take the first steps. In my own way, I began to consider what boarding the proverbial ship would look like without worrying about the details.

This journey to discovering the fullness of my call has been long and unexpected and continues to be ongoing. The more risks I take along the way, the more I find it to be good and holy, because the risks are faithful. I wonder: *How are you being faithful to the place you are planted? To the gifts and passions God has given you? What is the one thing you can't imagine not doing . . . and how are you faithfully living into that calling?*

Prayer: God who calls me and leads me in unexpected ways and places, may you help me to listen to your voice within me. In the quiet space of my life, may I listen—and hear—your voice calling me, leading me, and prompting me to live into the fullness of who you have created me to be. Amen.

Rev. Jen Tyler

When the angel came to her, he said, "Rejoice, favored one! The
Lord is with you! . . . Look! You will conceive and give birth to
a son, and you will name him Jesus." . . . Then Mary said, "I
am the Lord's servant. Let it be with me just as you have said."

—Luke 1:28, 31, 38

I have always felt a special kinship with Mary. I heard my call to ministry when I was sixteen years old. Mary was also a teenager when she was visited by the angel Gabriel. Many call stories in the Bible involve miraculous occurrences like this. Sarah heard the voice of God speaking through three visitors who said she would bear a child. Moses heard the voice of God calling from a burning bush. An angel visited Joseph in a dream.

My call story was less remarkable. As a high school student, I began to read the Bible, ask questions about what it said, and examine my faith. Through this ordinary experience, I felt an undeniable urge to serve God through pastoral ministry. There was no audible voice, angel, or vivid dream.

Sometimes a calling comes as a clear voice from God, but more often it comes as a gentle nudge, in the culmination of life experiences, or in our confrontation with a situation of great need that forces us to answer an immediate call to action. Sometimes the voice of God may come through the voice of friends, mentors, and colleagues.

While these stories might seem commonplace, God calls us in a multitude of ways. Ruth was called to a new place after a tragedy set her on a new path. Many of us feel called into new jobs, places, and relationships after loss and disappointment.

Esther was called to action when the Jewish people were threatened with persecution and death. She interceded on behalf of the people and saved them. Her call came as a response to injustice.

Mary Magdalene began following Jesus after he healed her from seven demons. Many people are called to work and volunteer in places and organizations that have had an impact on their personal lives.

God calls us in unique ways. Some stories might seem extraordinary and some commonplace. All stories of calling are miraculous because our Creator is inviting us to participate in the work of God.

Prayer: Dear God, open my heart to receive your call in whatever forms you send it. Give me the courage to say, "Here I am!" Help me feel your presence as I go to the people and places to which you have sent me. Amen.

Rev. Katie Goss Pearce

Ruth replied . . . "Wherever you go, I will go; and wherever you stay, I will stay. Your people will be my people, and your God will be my God. Wherever you die, I will die, and there I will be buried."

—*Ruth 1:16-17b*

It's a strange thing to be called by God. A beautiful but strange thing. It may come out of nowhere, jolting you into a new way of being. It may come through extended periods of focused prayer, providing the perfect lens that makes the fuzziness of life come into focus. However the call arrives, it is extended to us like a gift given without occasion, unexpected and undeserving. It is you I have been waiting for. It is God saying *It is you, the one I have known, the one I have loved. It is you I now call into a new existence, into a new partnership, into a new covenant.*

We have the choice, the option to accept or deny. And that period of consideration brings with it many questions. What will this mean, God? Where will this call take me? Who will go with me, and who will meet me when I get there? How will I know what to do? What if it all goes wrong? Unfortunately, in experiences of calling, most of the details remain unknown. But there the call sits, waiting to be accepted, to be opened up and explored, to be embraced and embodied. Oh, the excitement it holds. Oh, the anxiety it brings.

So, what will our answer be? I pray every day that I may answer as Ruth did: *Wherever you go, Lord, I will go. Wherever you stay, I will stay. Your people, they will be my people. When the world seems to be falling apart around me and I have nowhere else to go, may I go with you. When there are better options offered, easier paths to take, may I go with you. When I just can't stay to fight the daily battles of injustice, give me the strength and the courage to stay where you are. When the words I speak fall on deaf ears and the dreams I dream are crushed without care, may I be reminded that your people are my people. And when it feels like this calling is all but dead, may I lay it at your feet so that it may be raised again in your grace. Through it all, may I continue to say yes to this strange and beautiful calling.*

Prayer: O Lord, you call out, "Follow me." Give me the strength, the wisdom, and the grace to answer this call wherever it may lead. Amen.

Rev. Kristin Heiden

The apostles returned to Jesus. . . . Many people were coming and going, so there was no time to eat. He said to the apostles, "Come by yourselves to a secluded place and rest for a while." They departed in a boat by themselves for a deserted place.

—Mark 6:30-32

When the last call is over.
When the gavel strikes.
When the benediction is received.
When the classroom is emptied.
When the kids are tucked in.
When the work of our vocations comes to a stop, may we hear Jesus call to us: "Come . . . rest for a while."

As women in leadership, we often find ourselves the victims of our hectic schedules. Like the disciples, we have no time to eat, except maybe at our desk or in the car, but those meals are rarely satisfying. We are always pouring ourselves into work, colleagues, students, children, and others until we find we're empty from the constant strain of giving and going. It's not enough to be passionate, equipped, and talented in our vocations; we must also find time for renewal and rest in order to thrive.

These words from the Messiah to rest are, in fact, redeeming and saving words. They remind us we are human. We need times of rest so we can go beyond merely surviving our lives and vocations. We are no good to anyone if we are so worn out, so tired and haggard that we can hardly keep up, let alone lean into the goodness and abundance of meeting the needs of the world with our God-given talents and gifts—the very essence of vocational call.

Rather than finding ourselves taking on one more thing, completing one more task, or doing one more job at the end of the day, instead let us hear afresh these words from our Savior—indeed, from our Lord—as a command to rest our weary souls. "Come . . . rest for a while."

And when we have rested awhile, then we may return to wherever God has called us to serve, to overcome with courage, struggle with faithfulness, persist with heart, and resist with boldness.

Prayer: Lord, as you rested, so you call me to come away for a while to rest. Give me ears to hear your call and wisdom to sense my need to rest so that I may not only survive but also thrive in my life and vocation. Amen.

Rev. Danyelle Trexler

Struggle

In times of intense struggle, it can feel like God is a million miles away, distant and disconnected. Scripture tells us, though, that God is with us; in fact, Jesus is called "Emmanuel" which means just that. Especially during those times when we are hurting and sad, our plea becomes, "God, show me you are still here and that you care!"

Scripture affirms God's presence with us. We may not always be aware of it, but God is here, ever-present, providing us with grace, love, and strength. The struggles of this life are different for all of us. Although you may not find your exact struggle in the pages that follow, you will find within these devotions solidarity from other women who have walked or are walking similar paths.

When we are in the throes of our struggles, it becomes extremely hard for us to know where we are spiritually and emotionally. These devotions will help you find your footing. You will hear your questions, doubts, and yearnings echoed. In the experiences shared in the pages that follow, may you find some measure of grace in knowing you're not alone, but even more so in hearing God is walking with you through your difficult time. Your pain is genuine and matters a great deal to the God who loves you.

As you make your way through the struggle, ask God to show up for you. God wants you to know you are never alone, you have never been, and you never will be. Tell God that you need to feel the closeness that is promised. God is there, as close as your next breath. May these devotions help in your pursuit of that assuredness.

When my heart is weak,
    I cry out to you from the very ends of the earth.
Lead me to the rock that is higher than I am
    because you have been my refuge,
    a tower of strength in the face of the enemy.

—*Psalm 61:2-3*

When the demands of work, family, school—life in general—seem to mount up to the point that I can't cope any longer, the only thing I can do is cry out. I'm not talking about a quiet stream of tears. It's an ugly cry full of guttural moans and heaving sobs that leaves puffy, red eyes in its wake. It's as though my body can no longer contain or deny the weakness of my heart.

In those moments, it can feel like we are as far away from God as the ends of the earth. Like the psalmist, we might wonder where God is—and if God is listening—until the moment we cry out, "Listen to me, God!"

But whether our cries echo from the rafters or they whisper in our broken hearts, God is listening. God hears us, and God fills our wavering hearts with precisely what we need to make it through the trial at hand. God leads us to the "rock that is higher than I am." It could be anything, tangible or not, like a sudden windfall or a call from a friend or the moment you realize the worst is over. Whatever form it takes, the rock reminds us that when we put our faith in God, God leads us through the struggle.

And best of all, when we take refuge in God, we find we are newly equipped to overcome the struggle before us. God doesn't promise to take away all obstacles and challenges or that life will be free of hardship, but God will lead us through.

Like the psalmist, we must surrender ourselves over to God with an ugly, honest, heart-breaking cry. As we pour out our broken heart before God, God will pour in all we need to be made whole.

Prayer: Holy God, I lift up all that is broken and weary in my soul, for I know that nothing is too big for you to hold. When the way seems uncertain and I am most at a loss, let all of your goodness in my life be a light by which I may find the way through again. Thank you for loving me fiercely, even at my worst; rest with me now, until the storm recedes. Amen.

Rev. Shannon V. Trenton

I call on your name, Lord, from the depths of the pit. Hear my voice. Don't close your ear to my need for relief, to my cry for help. Come near to me on the day I call to you. Say to me, "Don't be afraid."

—Lamentations 3:55-57

When I began my career, over a decade ago, I received a lot of advice—both solicited and unsolicited. People gave me helpful pointers about where to live in my new city, the best professional networking events to attend with those who had cachet, and the most sought-after spots for a discreet business lunch. However, no one gave me advice on how to survive while in the pit.

What no one tells you about leadership is that things will change and with some change comes struggle. I was utterly unprepared when my professional and personal lives began to orbit on different planes. While I was thriving professionally, my personal life was falling apart. I was meeting all the professional standards for success, but my marriage, mental health, and physical health were crashing. I lived in a beautiful condo with a picturesque view; I attended the "right" events with the "right" people. I even knew the managers at the best restaurants in town. And yet, I found myself in the pit.

What no one tells you is that while in the pit, you will realize that your drive to live is greater than your fear. My life did seemingly fall apart: the marriage ended, my sister died unexpectedly, I became an adoptive single parent to my nephew, my father died, and then my ex-husband died. In the midst of unbearable grief, I was clinically depressed, super morbidly obese, and struggling to face the daily tasks of life. Still, I knew I was supposed to have a greater life and that this was not the end. One morning on my bedroom floor, I cried out to God, and She came near saying, "Do not fear."

What no one tells you is that in the most challenging circumstances you will find your authentic and best self. It was in the pit of life that I stopped seeking outside validation and began listening to my truth. Not only did I work to be my best public self but I committed to loving and taking care of the fragile parts of myself as well. I bathed in forgiveness and held myself with grace.

What no one tells is you is that one day you will look back and be amazed at yourself.

Prayer: Dear God, may I face every pit knowing that you are already there waiting for me to return to myself. Amen.

Rev. Dr. Theresa S. Thames

A Prayer for Transformation Through Struggle

Curled up, head in hands, tears streaming.
The days and nights run together.
Covered up, seeping with desperation.
Soaked pillows, hollow eyes.
There is no sense to be made.

The cry goes out, "How long, O Lord?"
How long?
How long . . .
Something changes.

Light peaks through.
Face begins to dry.
Sorrow gives way.
Little by little, God breaks in.
Bit by bit, healing starts.

Desperation turns to determination.
Sorrow to joy.
Weeping to dancing.
Life is renewed.

Merciful God, in this moment of struggle, let your comfort surround me. In time, wipe away my tears. Help me see beyond this despair. In your great mercy, turn my mourning into dancing. Amen.

Rev. Sarah A. Slack

Then he went a short distance farther and fell to the ground. He prayed that, if possible, he might be spared the time of suffering. He said, "Abba, Father, for you all things are possible. Take this cup of suffering away from me. However—not what I want but what you want."

—Mark 14:35-36

As a teenager, I struggled with depression. My life wasn't that hard, but I felt things deeply and personally. Everything felt like the worst thing I'd ever faced . . . because at fourteen it was. I had low self-esteem, I never thought I was good enough, and some days I was just sad.

The church was one place where I felt mostly accepted. While I was still a young Christian, I discovered the moment in Jesus's story when he prays in the garden. As a teenager with lots of feelings, I was drawn to this moment when the Savior of the world is broken and scared. He doesn't want to do the things ahead of him. He is sad too. And if Jesus can be sad and scared, maybe it's OK if I'm sad too.

This passage remains one I often turn to when things are not going well or when my depression decides to visit. I take some time to reflect upon Jesus's difficulties. I remember Jesus was scared of what he was about to face, and he feared enough to ask God for another way.

Perhaps, most importantly, he told God how he felt. "Take this cup," he cries. I imagine him pausing in the garden and deeply breathing in God's presence around him. After crying out and pausing, he is ready to embrace the fullness of God's love for humanity with all of who he was, human and divine, saying, "Not what I want but what you want."

God hears us when we cry out in our sadness, our fear, and our uncertainty. God knows the pain we feel when we face all kinds of struggles. God knows because God was there in Christ and with Christ, giving him the strength he needed to move forward and meet the challenges ahead. God is with us when we need to let out our fears, our uncertainty, and our sadness. God is there when we breathe in and are filled with the strength to face the next moment of our lives.

Prayer: Jesus, hear me as I echo your cry: take this cup from me. Fill me with your spirit that I may have the strength to say the next part of your prayer: not what I want, but what you want. Amen.

Rev. J. Paige Boyer

Why does your heart carry you away,
*   and why do your eyes flash,*
so that you turn your spirit against God,
*   and let such words go out of your mouth?*

—Job 15:12-13 NRSV

I remember the moment the call came: my father, who was battling cancer, had hours to live. Did I want to say good-bye over the phone? I found a quiet escape and prayed, saying the words I knew I needed to say. I took a deep breath, wiped my tears, and waited.

I had so many questions at the end of what was, at best, a complicated relationship. I wondered how I got there. That summer, I lost more people than I had in my entire life before that. With each passing week, the news got worse, and the death stung deeper.

"Why?!" I yelled as I lifted my head to the sky. "Why are you doing this to me?!"

I had always been taught that God would carry us in difficult times. Yet when I needed God most, I felt so alone. I waffled between numbness and overwhelming, crippling grief. Longing for good news, I opened my Bible to a random page. I looked down to see Job, the man who lost everything. He lost his wife, his children, his livelihood . . . and for what? So God could win a bet with Satan? I started reading where my finger had landed: "Why does your heart carry you away?"

This only made me more angry. In the midst of my struggle, God, that's what you have for me? Yet I knew better. I knew God was with me. I knew it was happenstance to land on these words, but it was also an invitation to let God console me. And so I wept.

Sometimes, weeping is all we have. In those moments, God is with us. When we cry out, when we are grieving, when we are struggling with grief too heavy to name, God is with us.

As I wept that day, I gave God my struggles, my yelling, my anger, and my grief. I wept until I was too tired to weep anymore.

When I woke the next day, I was unable to shake the idea that this is what Mary and the disciples must have felt like when the grief of Jesus's death overwhelmed them, before they discovered the joy that would come with the Resurrection.

Sometimes, waiting can be the worst part. Yet even in the midst of the worst, even if nothing is OK, we can know that, one day, it will be. It will be, because God is with us.

Prayer: Mighty and merciful God, draw near to me in the depths of my despair. Hold me close when I lose my center and help me focus on you. May I never lose sight of the ways you are with me, pouring in to me and guiding me—on the good days and on the worst ones. Amen.

Rev. Jen Tyler

A Prayer for the Unplanned End of Breastfeeding

Holy Comforter, I come to you at the end of this treasured connection I have experienced with my child through breastfeeding.

I did not think that the last time we latched would be the last.

Sometimes I wished that I didn't have to be depended on so much to be a main food source, and other times I longed to be reunited with my child when we were separated.

And now, here I am Lord, unlatched.

Wrap me in your arms as I grieve this loss. Thank you for the time I did have to comfort, nurture, and provide for my child through my body.

I step into this unknown territory with you, still a parent and still your child, latched and unlatched during various seasons. I pray for your loving guidance so I may see new ways in which you are calling me to comfort, to nurture, and to provide for my child. Amen.

Rev. Melissa Engel

*But Moses' hands grew tired. So they took a stone and put it
under Moses so he could sit down on it. Aaron and Hur held up
his hands, one on each side of him so that his hands remained
steady until sunset.*

—*Exodus 17:12*

We all struggle at least some of the time. It's a universal human phenomenon. It may be physical, mental, relational, or spiritual, but no one lives without struggle.

Knowing this, you might think we would see a struggle coming toward us and think, "Oh, hello! I thought you might come today. You're not my favorite thing, to be honest, but such is life." Instead, when struggle shows up, we often think we are the only ones, somehow doomed with the dark clouds of struggle, while everyone else sails through life on a rainbow. What's worse is that many of us have gotten the message that our struggle means we are wrong or weak or incompetent, that the very existence of struggle in our lives means we have failed in some way.

I love this story from Exodus because it's so boring and human and real. The Israelites are fighting the Amalekites, and as long as Moses's hands are raised, the Israelites win the battle; but if he lowers his hands, they start to lose. This wouldn't be an issue, but Moses's arms get tired and he can't hold them up anymore. What an absurd reason for a whole people to lose a battle: because their leader's arms got tired! He literally has the power of God in his hands, but he can't hold them up because he's tired!

But God doesn't chastise Moses for being weak. Instead, when Moses's arms are tired, his friends hold them up. Maybe he is incompetent. Maybe his weakness is the cause of the struggle. But God never intended for him to lead alone, and God doesn't intend for us to pull ourselves through this life alone either. Our reliance on other people is built into the very fabric of our bodies—otherwise, our arms wouldn't get tired, and neither would our hearts or our eyes or our voices. So next time you're struggling, instead of berating yourself for your weakness, look for whom God might have put into your life to hold you up. It might not be the people you imagined, but someone will offer you their strength until you can hold yourself up again.

Prayer: God, thank you for making me to be in relationship with others. When I struggle, help me look beyond myself for strength. Amen.

Rev. Elizabeth Ingram Schindler

I raise my eyes toward the mountains.
Where will my help come from?
My help comes from the Lord,
the maker of heaven and earth.

—Psalm 121:1-2

Recall what it feels like, deep in your bones, to struggle. There's a tenseness of muscles and an ache in the pit of the stomach. There's exhaustion, each task weighing your soul down. There's a weight on your shoulders that comes from carrying the worry about what might happen next.

How does your body carry struggle? When I struggle with a problem, with a person, or with wondering what will happen next, I often experience tunnel vision. I can only see that one issue; all else fades into the background, unimportant in the midst of my struggle.

But, when I consider the words of this psalm, my struggles are no longer front and center. The psalmist reminds me God creates and makes things new.

I raise my eyes from my struggle to see the beauty of a sunset.

I raise my eyes from the problem demanding all of my attention and energy and catch the wonder of a bird in flight.

I raise my eyes, and God is there: in a person's smile, in a helping hand, in a breath taken, in knowing all I need to do is the next right thing, whatever that might be.

My problem, my struggle, whatever it might be, is still there. But by raising my eyes I see God's creation all around, and the burden on my shoulders begins to ease. The ache in my stomach and knots in my back release. God's great love for each of us is just waiting to be seen. Our eyes are made for looking up and realizing that help comes from the Lord.

A prayer exercise:

Breathe in deeply.
Breathe out deeply.
Repeat as needed.

Roll your shoulders forward,
then up to your ears,
then settle them as far down your back as possible,
Sit up straight and expectant.

Breathe in God. Breathe out God.
Lift your eyes . . .
to the mountains,
to the horizon,
to the ceiling,
and pray . . .

Prayer: Holy God, train my eyes to lift to you. I know my help in this time of struggle comes from you. Protect me as I take this breath, guide me in my next right step on my journey, as I remember you are with me, from now to forever from now. I pray, looking up, looking to you, and in the name of your son, Jesus Christ, God-with-us. Amen.

Rev. Megan E. Thompson

～ A Prayer in the Midst ～
of Technical Difficulties

**(Or, God, I have already smashed the patriarchy today,
please don't make me smash the printer too.)**

"O Lord, you have searched me and known me."[1] But I wish you would search and know this machinery so I don't have to pull out my hair trying to figure it out. And yes, I already tried shutting it down and turning it back on again.

I have important things to do, and so I just need your wisdom dealing with technology so I can go about the rest of my day

   because this day will not stop!

These frustrations build and build, and I don't have the time or the energy for it. Help me transform this moment into a space for breath and reconnection. Soothe my aggravated nerves and help me see clearly in the midst of the mess. Amen.

Rev. Shannon E. Sullivan

The LORD is your keeper; the LORD is your shade at your right hand. The sun shall not strike you by day, nor the moon by night. The LORD will keep you from all evil; he will keep your life. The LORD will keep your going out and your coming in from this time on and forevermore.

—Psalm 121:5-8 NRSV

My kitchen table has crumbs on it. There is a baby seat in the bathroom, a Bumbo on the kitchen counter, an ExerSaucer in the dining room, and toys scattered on the living room rug. Several days, worth of mail has piled up in the entryway beneath the mail slot. The dishwasher is full of clean dishes, and the sink is full of dirty ones.

The struggle is real. And it is daily.

As a woman in leadership, I fully expected to struggle against the patriarchy, to fight the system on a regular basis, to smash glass and stained glass ceilings whenever I could, but I never anticipated the struggle of home life being so darn hard. I didn't plan for the challenge of keeping clean clothes, the ever-encroaching dust bunnies, or the tornado-like mess of baby clutter. I never dreamed meal planning or cooking would be so exhausting.

But, all of a sudden, it is. I expected home life to be easier, leaving me free to take on the challenges of professional leadership. The reality, though, is that most days, saving the world takes a backseat to getting the baby fed, spending time with my spouse, and making sure we all have clean underwear for the next day.

Life has those big, beautiful moments, but mostly it's made up of mundane things. We might imagine the struggles to be against the big things like patriarchy and sexism, but usually, it's the ordinary, everyday, get-it-done stuff. The going out and the coming in. Day and night. Laundry and piles of mail. Dirty kitchen tables and sinks of dishwater.

The good news is that God is in the business of making mundane things holy. The crumbs of a table can nourish us, sustain us, and strengthen us. Water can be transformed to remind us we are part of a larger story. So keep walking, sister, around the toy-scattered floor. Keep moving, sister, through the daily struggle. Keep your head high, sister, for you are not alone.

Prayer: God, I expect to find you in the extraordinary, but I so often encounter you in the ordinary. Open my eyes to your daily, sustaining presence. Amen.

Rev. Brandi Tevebaugh Horton

Be strong! Be fearless! Don't be afraid and don't be scared by
your enemies, because the LORD your God is the one who marches
with you. {God} won't let you down, and {God} won't abandon
you."

—Deuteronomy 31:6

Have you ever had a moment when you all of a sudden realize there is nowhere left to turn and you are all alone? There is no fearless leader ahead of you.

That moment when you feel like the world is on your shoulders and there is no one else to help carry or lighten the load.

That moment when you look around and realize everyone has left you.

That feeling of abandonment in the pit of your stomach.

The task ahead seems too daunting or too overwhelming.

You start second-guessing whether you heard God correctly in the first place.

Panic wells up within you and all you want to do is find a way out of this.

I imagine the Israelites might have felt something like that when they heard Moses say he was not going with them into the Promised Land. Moses quickly reminds them God is going to be with them. With strength and encouragement, Moses reminds them they are not abandoned. God is with them.

Sometimes life happens and it leaves us feeling abandoned by others and—maybe especially—by God. We wonder why God saved one person we prayed for and allowed another to die. We wonder why God intervened in one situation while remaining silent in another. In fact, sometimes we feel that God has let us and others down. It can be a struggle to see God working in the middle of our messy lives.

In the midst of uncertainty, Moses reminds the Israelites that God still marches with them. They do not need to fear. They do not face the moment or the future alone. Sometimes the only comfort in which we can rest comes from claiming the promise made to the Israelites: God will not let us down—God has not abandoned us!

Even when we may not feel God's love, hear God's voice, or see God's movement in the middle of the struggle . . . God is still there right beside us.

Prayer: Ever-present God, even when I feel alone, you are there. Help me feel your presence in uncertain moments and uncertain places. Help me be strong and fearless and to go where you lead me. Amen.

Rev. Rebecca L. Laird

∼ A Prayer for Infertility ∼

Holy God, You have placed a mothering heart inside me, and yet, not equipped that same body to be able to grow a child. Protect me from the unhelpful advice, well-meaning platitudes, and downright stupid things other people say. Provide me a measure of your peace that passes understanding, because this is past understanding. Amen.

Rev. Sarah Karber

∼ A Prayer in the Middle ∼ of a Miscarriage

Jesus, when you were in the garden of Gethsemane, you were in such anguish; it was as though great drops of blood fell from your body.[2] I am in great anguish now because of the blood falling out of my body. Blood that was my baby—is my baby? I don't even know anymore. All I know is that my baby is leaving me. I am in such pain. My whole body aches; my contractions echo from my womb throughout my body. But that pain is nothing compared to the contractions of my heart. How can this life be gone from mine already? And how can I go on without that life?

Give me back my baby, God.
I am overcome with grief.
Amen.

Rev. Shannon E. Sullivan

*God has generously granted you the privilege, not only of
believing in Christ but also of suffering for Christ's sake. You
are having the same struggle that you saw me face and now hear
that I'm still facing.*

—*Philippians 1:29-30*

Y ou're not the only one." This phrase epitomizes my experience as a
member of an ecumenical organization called Young Clergy Women
International. Through Facebook groups, online articles, and people I
have met in person at conferences and at regional meet-ups, time and time
again, as I have shared struggles with these colleagues, I've heard, "You're
not the only one."

Leadership has the potential to be isolating. Sometimes when we struggle, whether in leading our organization or in dealing with challenges in
our personal lives, it is tempting to think, "Everyone else has figured out
how to cope with this, and I'm the only one who hasn't." I take great
comfort in my supportive colleagues who share they are facing the same
difficulties. Sometimes they've survived and offer wisdom from their experience, and other times they only say they're in the midst of suffering the
same struggle.

Paul's letter to the church at Philippi offered instruction and encouragement in the face of real challenges. He wanted those early Christians
to know that they were not alone in their struggles and suffering. He had
faced the same struggles.

Sometimes it seems like people expect following Jesus will remove every
trial and tribulation from your life. We know from Paul's experience that
sometimes it is by following Christ that we enter into great adversity. The
circumstances in which I live are very different than Paul's, but I have faced
difficulties because of following Christ. In each struggle, I have turned to
others, who have said to me, "You're not the only one."

God blessed me with others who would bear witness to my life and ministry, and in doing so, help me survive the most difficult moments. It is a gift to have others willing to bear witness to our suffering. Not simply to observe from a distance and to offer us pity, but to be present in that moment of suffering, to come alongside, name the pain, and say, "You're not the only one."

Prayer: Holy Spirit, you are with me always. Surround me now so that I may feel the way in which you bear witness to my life. In all my struggles, suffering, and powerlessness, please be with me and bear this with me, so that I would remember that I am not alone.

Rev. Sarah Harrison-McQueen

"My God, My God, why have you forsaken me?"

—Mark 15:34

The loneliness was palpable. It was the first time my kids were away since the divorce. My home was eerily quiet except for the occasional sobs I let slip as I cried myself to exhaustion. After a week, it was finally time to drive to the meeting place—that neutral halfway point where divorced parents meet to swap kids at the end of visits.

Driving down the interstate, keenly aware I looked like a hot mess, I heard the slow build-up of the song "I Will Survive." As the beat picked up, I cranked the volume. Suddenly, I was engaged in an epic duet. Without a care in the world for being off-key and out of tune or how ridiculous I looked to passing cars, I sang with all my heart the timeless words: "As long as I know how to love, I know I'll stay alive . . . I will survive."[3]

When I read the words from the cross, they remind me Jesus is a God who feels my feels, thinks my thinks, and can walk with me through the messiest parts of my life, primarily through those dark valleys. I don't have the time for or need of a god who judges from on high. I need Jesus, who knows the sting of betrayal, the crushing agony of feeling abandoned, and the strength to endure to the end. I need Jesus, who proves that even after the darkest days—when it seems evil has won—still Easter comes.

As followers of Jesus, we are Easter people. We believe the darkness does not overcome the light. We believe in a savior who defeated the powers of sin and death. We believe in a God who does not abandon us to our most profound hurts, does not leave us alone in our pain, does not lose hope in us. The struggle is real. It's like living every day as though it's Good Friday. But remember, God does not abandon you in your struggles. God is with you.

That day in the car was a turning point in my post-divorce struggle. My life didn't suddenly become all sunshine and rainbows, but I had a renewed sense of peace and strength. I was always a person who enjoyed life, who laughed easily and smiled at strangers—and I would be again. The darkness of divorce would not steal the light from my life. I will survive because Easter comes.

Prayer: God of light and love, pour out your Holy Spirit on me this day that I may endure, that I may know your love deep in my bones and continue to move forward. Amen.

Rev. Danyelle Trexler

⌒ A Prayer for Helplessness ⌒

Almighty God, how can I possibly do this? How can I move forward, knowing that nothing is the same? It all seems too much—much more than I can bear. Hide me under the shadow of your wings. In this moment, I feel utterly helpless. Cover me with your peace and give me the strength needed for what is to come. If it be your will, take this burden from me. Even Jesus asked for the cup to pass. Let me feel your presence by my side, and to trust that you, in your faithfulness, will be with me always, through all things. Amen.

Rev. Jennifer Zeigler Medley

⌒ A Prayer for Loneliness ⌒

Almighty God, even though I know in my head that there is nowhere I can go to escape your presence, at times I feel so alone.

Surround me with individuals and community to journey with me on my best days and my worst days and to show me that I am not alone.

When isolation and loneliness threaten to overwhelm me, wrap me in your loving arms and help me find peace in your presence.

When I feel unworthy, instill in me the truth and joy of my identity as a beloved child of God. Amen.

Rev. Laura-Allen Kerlin

When God began to create the heavens and the earth—the earth
was without shape or form, it was dark over the deep sea, and
God's wind swept over the waters.

—Genesis 1:1-2

R ecently our son was diagnosed with high-functioning autism. At first,
I felt relief. After a year and a half of evaluations and late-night mus-
ings of whether he had autism, now we knew the answer. There was relief
that we could finally move forward with a plan of action.

But soon the relief wore off as the fear and questions set in. Was it my
fault for not catching the signs earlier? Was there more I could have done
to help him get a better start in life? How do you explain what autism is
to friends and family who know him? What will this mean for him and my
family for the long-term future? To live in the uncertainty this diagnosis
brings is difficult and scary. I put on the brave face that everything will be
all right, but in the back of my mind I wonder, *Will it be?*

As a pastor, I counsel those who are going through different struggles. I
pray with them and remind them God is with them. Now I was beginning
to wonder where God was at in the midst of my struggle.

In the first creation account in the book of Genesis, the author recounts
how God made the world. Popular belief is that God created the world out
of nothing, but a closer reading reveals there was something already here.[4]
What was here was chaos and water. But God was still able to create beauty
and order out of the uncertain existence. In the midst of my own struggle
and chaos, in a sea of unanswered questions, I began to trust that God was
in the middle of my uncertainty, too.

God is at work creating something beautiful out of our chaos. We may
not know what beauty will emerge, and we won't have all the answers; but
we see how the Holy Spirit swept over the deep waters of creation, and
that same divine presence will sweep over the deep waters of our souls. In

that awareness is the peace and reassurance that God is with us every step of the way.

Prayer: God of creation, as your Spirit swept over the deep waters of chaos, forming your beautiful creation, may your Spirit be present in the deep waters of my chaotic struggle. May you breathe life into the midst of my uncertainty and bring beauty out of this struggle. Amen.

Rev. Elizabeth R. Taylor

What do workers gain from all their hard work? I have observed
the task that God has given human beings.

—Ecclesiastes 3:9-10

The ever-present, overwhelming, busyness of life collapsed onto me a few years ago just before Lent started. During particular moments of stress and defeat, I found myself repeating the same response: "I am busy." From a simple "how are you" to an invitation to coffee to requests for help, the answer was the same: "I'm busy." It was then I decided to take away one word from my vocabulary. Not to speak or even think it for forty days. During the season of Lent, I was giving up the word *busy*.

One word had started to define my whole life and become an exasperated response to all inquiries about my day and feelings. The gift of Lent was that for forty days I had a defined period to be intentional in the endeavor to omit this word from my daily speak.

In that time, the discipline taught me some valuable lessons. First, everyone is competing to be busy. It's as though we wear it as a badge of honor. Second, I'm not that busy, especially when I compare my life with its many blessings to that of others who do not share the same privileges. Third, my anxiety and hyped-up feelings about work and schedules distracted me from the essentials, like relationships and self-care. And finally, *busy* had replaced opportunities for prayer and reflection that would cultivate a stronger relationship with God, myself, and others.

We must trust that God knows the busyness of our days. When we struggle to do everything all on our own, too frequently we lose ourselves. Rather than draw closer to God in prayer, we allow ourselves to be drawn deeper into the busyness and an out-of-control lifestyle. And yet, God remains faithful. Constantly calling out, trying to get our attention, to remind us our *busy* is not always about the work of grace and love. When we are so very busy, we miss out on opportunities for transformation and for serving God in life-giving ways. The task God has given us is to be people of abundant grace in a broken world. May we recall our work is not to be busy but to press on in a relationship with God.

Prayer: Gracious Redeemer, may my busy *be transformed into the work of grace and love. Restore my soul and schedule that I may gain righteousness. Amen.*

Rev. Blair Tolbert

A Prayer for Starting Over

Lord, why am I being asked to start over? Again.
You know how I hate this, how my soul recoils at the thought.
I want to run far from this.

I am tired of being the positive one.
I am tired of being strong.
In fact, I am just plain tired.

I had begun to really love this place—her people, her strange charm.
I know who I am here.
I know what is expected.

And my family, Lord, my family.
They have grown roots, beautiful roots.
How will they not bear scars from this change?

My soul groans with sighs too deep for words. Help me, for I can barely
breathe.

Be my breath.
Remind me that you go before me and that even if I flee you will go with me.
Strengthen me for the days ahead.
Be my words. Be my courage. Be my peace.
Amen.

Rev. Leslie Stephens

But God chose what the world considers foolish to shame the wise. God chose what the world considers weak to shame the strong. And God chose what the world considers low-class and low-life—what is considered to be nothing—to reduce what is considered to be something to nothing.

—*1 Corinthians 1:27-28*

All around us are signs of the world's brokenness. These signs include significant systemic problems like racism, sexism, and heterosexism, and all the myriad ways those show up in our daily lives through microaggressions at work and home. They include bodies broken through disease and unequal access to health care. They include spirits broken from being passed over, beaten down, ignored, and underappreciated. They include addiction, sexual harassment, and debt. They include all the ways we have failed or fallen short. We are unsatisfied and frustrated when we see these signs. We may feel like we are not up to the task of being part of healing the brokenness, especially when we can so clearly see brokenness in our own lives.

But.

But brokenness is not the only story we have to tell. Brokenness is not all there is. And we don't have to be whole for God to need us for the important work of healing. In Paul's first letter to the Corinthians, he does not hide the fact that life and ministry have been difficult for him. His story includes imprisonment, pain, and infighting with other followers of Christ. Elsewhere in 1 Corinthians, he talks about how he has been harassed, insulted, even considered to be "scum of the earth, the waste that runs off everything" (4:12-13). He knows what it is like to see the signs of the world's brokenness and come face to face with his own.

And.

And God chose him, not because of his strength, but because through weakness, God exposes the truth that worldly strength is nothing. God chooses you, too. Not because life is perfect for you or because you are perfect. But because God ignores the world's message of wrongness to proclaim the truth: you are right. God, who is with you in the brokenness, whispers to you that the brokenness will be reduced to nothing. And that you are something. You are someone. Someone essential and loved, someone who will be healed and who will help others see signs of wholeness instead.

Prayer: God who loves me even when I worry I am unlovable, erase the signs of brokenness in my life. Replace them instead with messages of your wisdom and strength to carry me through, so I may become a sign to others of your promise of wholeness. Amen.

Rev. Dr. Emily A. Peck-McClain

When Rachel realized that she could bear Jacob no children,
Rachel became jealous of her sister and said to Jacob, "Give me
children! If you don't, I may as well be dead."

—Genesis 30:1

A single blue line on a stick. Not pregnant.

There have been times in my life when I have breathed a sigh of relief at this news. And there have been other times when I have felt my heart closing in on itself. Another month of trying. Another month of waiting.

Scripture offers us several stories of women struggling with their fertility. Sarah. Rachel. Hannah. Elizabeth. All of them are eventually blessed with sons who hold great destinies. They are patriarchs, dreamers, leaders, and prophets. The wonder of a womb that can birth a miracle who changes the face of the earth.

Rachel would eventually give birth twice. Her firstborn she named Joseph, meaning "he adds," for how he added to her joy. But her second born, for whom the birth was a struggle that she would die from, she wanted to name Ben-oni, "my suffering son." Jacob changed his name to Benjamin, meaning "son of my right hand," a name for someone who is a blessing. It was out of Rachel's suffering that blessing came.

We are blessed in the age of The Pill that the meaning of our lives does not hinge on whether we have children. We can birth strength into the world through different means. But the desire to have children remains strong for many women. The means it takes to adopt, conceive, foster, or birth always involves thorough testing of who we are. Through the pain of waiting and hoping, expecting and praying, we find an inner strength that we would never have dreamed possible. In the pain of being a part of something larger than ourselves, we rest in the arms of God, who carries us when we are weak.

There was a time for me when there were two lines instead of one. And my tears of relief and anxiety flowed. My heart closed in on itself and opened up wide. What a gift, to carry a life within me. It was not going to be easy. The world as I knew it had changed. But what was to come would add to my joy as it added to my struggles.

Prayer: Holy God, thank you for the sacrifices the women in my life made for me. I would not be where I am if not for them. Help me care for and mentor the children in my life, that they may know how loved they are and be inspired to do great things. Amen.

Rev. Heather Dorr

A Prayer for When Bedtime with Children Is Stressful

Lord, help me remember that I love these children.
Remind me that I love them with everything I am.

Give me patience.
Give me peace.
Give me kind words.
Lord, help me make it through these long moments,
that we might all rest and wake tomorrow to new beginnings.
Amen.

Rev. Anjie Peek Woodworth

A Prayer for When You Just Can't

God who is with us when we have no words. . . .

Amen.

Listen, God; we are despised! Turn their insults to us back on their heads and make them like plunder in a captive land. Don't forgive their iniquity or blot out their sins from your sight. They have thrown insults at the builders!

—Nehemiah 4:4-5

Those words sound so very good.

To the tested, long-standing, and hardest working of leaders, Nehemiah's plea to God sounds just right. Let every "I told you so" or "if only" or "you should have done it differently" be silenced. Dig us out from under heaping mounds of doubt and ridicule and mockery. Free the ones building your Kingdom and bury the enemies.

Go get 'em, God!

There's a part of leadership no one talks about much. It's not the exciting, successful part. It's not the moments that make you look good or that clearly and effortlessly exemplify the presence of God. It's the side where there's pain, fear, and struggle. And it's in every leader's story.

Nehemiah left a high position with the king in comfortable circumstances to rebuild the walls of Jerusalem. His call was validated in many ways, including the tremendous response of the Israelites: "Let's start rebuilding!" But after a burst of success came the ones who sought to tear it down. Halfway through the project, Nehemiah became more than a wall builder. He shifted his focus to protecting his call from God and fighting for the success he had already built.

The attack Nehemiah endured is the same today. Opposition often follows success. Growth always threatens those who wish to cut it off. Goodness and beauty are things to be treasured and protected. The real strength of Nehemiah's work is his response to his enemies.

No! You will not tear down what has been built up in the name of God. You will not be allowed to triumph over God's people again. We are the

Lord's, and this work will be done. That which we are building is not ours alone, but it is ours because it was God's first.

You're wrong, dear enemy.

Prayer: O Lord, fuel me further still as a leader. Give me the words to speak back to those who tear down. Give me the courage to go deeper still in the struggle that is the reality of my call. Amen.

Rev. Sarai Case

*Many Samaritans in that city believed in Jesus because of the
woman's word when she testified, "He told me everything I've
ever done." So when the Samaritans came to Jesus, they asked
him to stay with them, and he stayed there two days. Many more
believed because of his word.*

—John 4:39-41

He told me everything I've ever done." Those words are powerful testimony by a woman whose name is unknown to any of us, except as "the woman at the well." The little bit we know of her life is that it was full of pain and moments of doubt. Her story could be ours. It could be the story of every woman in our life. It could be the story of every female leader who has struggled to pave the way for other women to lead.

So often, others claim to know everything about our story, everything we have ever done, and they shape that knowledge for whatever purpose they see fit. They will twist the beauty and pain and complexity of our lives into one or two laudatory or accusatory sentences for all the world to regard as a badge of honor or shame. Our most profound struggles are all too often brought forward as shameful weakness rather than strength born amidst chaos.

We know our own stories; we spend both time and heart to claim them, the rough edges and the smooth. Jesus also knows our stories—each mundane, chaotic, beautiful, heartbreaking moment. He could tell us everything that we have ever done, but he does not use our actions against us or manipulate them beyond recognition. Instead, as he did with the woman at the well, he offers us living water and helps us see that our stories are intermingled with the light and life of his story.

The woman's testimony of her encounter with Christ in the midst of her own story made her people take notice of this man she claimed was the Messiah. She knew the risk—that they would not look beyond what they thought they knew about her life to listen—but she also understood that this new part of her story had to be told. Everyone needed to know that Jesus was there to offer something so incredible for them through his grace and truth. Because she bravely witnessed to them, they went to see for themselves, and many came to believe. A new chapter was written into their stories too.

Prayer: Gracious God, give me the words to tell my own story, weave my story seamlessly into yours. Help me lead others to know that Jesus brings light and life to all, no matter what twists and turns their stories contain. Amen.

Rev. Shannon Rodenberg

~ A Prayer for the Illness of a Parent ~

Spirit of Love, Grace, and Healing, I call on you in my hour of need, seeking wisdom and guidance, needing comfort, hope, and peace. Most of all, I seek healing for the one who raised me.

Whenever I was sick as a child, those arms enfolded me, providing comfort and love. Now, I feel helpless as I seek to become one who gives care.

May your presence enable me to share the same comfort and love, which I seek now from you. Wrap your arms of love around both of us. Bestow your healing spirit on my parent who is suffering, and work through all those providing care that they may be your hands and feet. Renew my strength so that I may continually lift my petitions to you and bear witness to your Spirit at work.

Bless me now, O God, and remember the one I hold dear. Amen.

Rev. Jennifer Zeigler Medley

~ A Prayer Before Surgery ~

Lord, you are the Great Physician, and I call on you to guide the surgeon and medical team who will be caring for me today. Bless them with the wisdom, compassion, and skill needed to make this surgery successful. I give thanks for the calling that led them to this place and to this moment to be my care team. Watch over me this day, fill me with peace, and ease every bit of fear or nervousness I may feel. Bring me through surgery and to a quick and full recovery. Amen.

Rev. Jennifer Zeigler Medley

Jesus said to him, "'If you can do anything'? All things are possible for the one who has faith." At that the boy's father cried out, "I have faith; help my lack of faith!"

—*Mark 9:23-24*

In a time of urgent need, parents finds themselves caught between belief and unbelief. In the case of this story, it is a father and son, but it could easily be a mother and daughter, or any parent and child linked through a fierce familial bond of love. It could be anyone caught in overwhelming circumstances outside their control. This particular parent, desperate to help his child, pleads with Jesus for help.

"If you can do anything, help us."

Jesus's answer seems to offer little comfort: "'If you can do anything,'?" he challenges. "All things are possible for the one who has faith." If this were scripted dialogue, the father might launch into a long and pious monologue about his faithfulness. But, the gospel is about real life. And the father replies as any parent might: "I have faith; help my lack of faith!"

In one breath, this confession pierces all façades of superficial piety, revealing the heartbreaking and hopeful truth of faith lived in the midst of struggle: "I have faith; help my lack of faith." Jesus honors this honesty with action and heals the boy.

In doing so, Jesus validates the profound truth that you can have faith and doubt at the same time. God will begin with the faith you have, even the smallest kernel, but that's all that is needed.

Instead of pretending always to have it together, a faithful leader will acknowledge there are times when the internal struggle to have faith in the face of trying circumstances is hard. Many times, we struggle with guilt or, worse, shame at the realization our faith isn't rock solid. But here in this passage, we discover Jesus comes to those who honestly and earnestly seek him out in the midst of life's most significant challenges, even when our faith is only holding by a thread. When we bare ourselves to Jesus, we are blessed by his healing presence. As leaders, the struggles will come, we will doubt ourselves and God's faith in us, but we need only to remember that the same grace given that long-ago day comes to us too.

Prayer: God of vulnerability and power, as I face the circumstances of this day, I confess to you, "I have faith; help my lack of faith." Reveal your healing presence in the midst of my struggle, fortify my faith with your love, and carry my weakness in your nurturing arms. Remind me of your promises and help me bear witness to my faith in you with honesty and love. Amen.

Rev. Colleen Hallagan Preuninger

*But all shall be well, and all shall be well, and all manner of
thing shall be well."*[5]

—*Julian of Norwich*

As a hospital chaplain, I spend a lot of time with people for whom all is not well. Their stories are often heartbreaking: their bodies are not well, and frequently, as a result, their emotional lives are not well, their relationships are not well, and their souls are not well. To say to them, "all shall be well," feels insensitive to the pain they are experiencing. And yet, those are precisely the words that Julian of Norwich heard from Jesus in a vision during a time when she suffered from a grave illness and was prepared to die. Instead of death, she experienced God speaking to her, offering visions of unending love. God reminded her that although there are reasons to worry, reasons to feel exhausted by life's struggles, God will provide for us.

The first time I heard these words was in a song we performed in my church choir. From the moment I first sang her words, they struck a chord deep within my soul. It felt counterintuitive to say "all shall be well" at a time in my life when all was very much not well. But something was grounding and affirming in repeatedly singing that phrase against a simple yet powerful melody. Julian's visions remind us that amid all of our struggles, God provides us unending love, hope, and peace, no matter what. Indeed, all shall be well.

We all have those moments, seasons, and even years when all is not well. We face struggles that churn up those gut-wrenching feelings of unrest, times when we cry out to God for peace and wholeness and rest amid pain, uncertainty, and chaos. One of the hardest things to do is to sit with that "unwellness," to realize we are unable to fix it and, yet still, to find some measure of peace. Julian's visions remind us peace isn't the absence of struggle; rather peace is remaining grounded in the strength of our faith, in a belief that tells us God is our ultimate source of peace and that, through God, all shall indeed be well.

Prayer: O God, I seek your peace amid life's struggles. I pray that although the struggles continue and at times seem to come without ceasing, I may experience ultimate grounding in the circle of your peace. I pray all shall be well, and all shall be well, and all manner of things shall be well.

Rev. Dr. Christina L. Wright

～ A Prayer for One Day ～

I have crawled through grief.
I have cried a river of sadness.
I have raged in anger.
I have shouted in bitterness.
I have no peace.
My pain recycles.
Crawling.
Crying.
Raging.
Shouting.
Nothing.
Where are you, God?
Then I walked.
Then I smiled.
Then I calmed.
Then I sang.
Then I discovered a new cycle.
Walking.
Smiling.
Calming.
Singing.
Discovering.
O God, are you with me?
One day I will run with gladness.
One day I will laugh from my soul.
One day I will shout with joy.
One day I will be happy again.
One day the pain of this struggle will be over.
I know you were there all along, God.
Amen.

Rev. Danyelle Trexler

"As surely as the LORD your God lives," {*the widow of Zare-phath*} *replied, "I don't have any food; only a handful of flour in a jar and a bit of oil in a bottle. Look at me. I'm collecting two sticks so that I can make some food for myself and my son. We'll eat the last of the food and then die." Elijah said to her, "Don't be afraid!"*

—*1 Kings 17:12-13a*

I believe in miracles. I just don't believe in miracles for myself anymore. I preach a God of abundance. Only I find it increasingly difficult to find that abundance in my own life. I often feel like the widow of Zarephath, whose response to a stranger asking for food is to tell him simply and bitterly: "I don't have anything. I'm going to die." I know that bitterness, even if I don't know that literal hunger.

This episode in Scripture comes during a famine. Elijah was in hiding, led to a place where he would have food and water, but then even that water dried up. Each step of the way, every time he felt lost and fearful, "the Lord's word" came to him, directing him anew. But this was not the case for the widow of Zarephath, at least, not that Scripture tells us. We just meet her collecting sticks, at the end of her hope. And then Elijah, who must have looked a little worse for the wear, and who was a foreigner, showed up wanting to be fed.

The widow didn't dance around her pain. She wasn't apologetic. She told Elijah she had nothing left but one meager meal. She was going to feed her son and then wait for death. And Elijah's response? It is strange. He tells her not to be afraid and then repeats his desire for food even after hearing she doesn't have enough for him. But perhaps his words were gentle, cutting to the heart of the truth of the widow's fear. She had her son, yes. But she felt so very alone. But maybe she wasn't after all. Maybe the God this strange person represented was with her after all.

I've felt alone often, especially in these times of struggle, but it turns out that God has been with me. I hold on to the appearance of strangers offering words of comfort and hope. Even if I am all out of hope myself, others are holding on to it for me, even people I have never met. And that is where I find abundance, where I taste miracles again. But it also reminds me that even in our struggles, we can be that voice of possibility for someone else. We can dispel fear and urge others to take a risk. And in that risk, maybe even experience miracles again.

Prayer: As surely as you live, O God, bring me back to life. In the midst of my struggles, send me messengers of hope. In the midst of my fear, show me how to live into your abundant life. Amen.

Rev. Shannon E. Sullivan

"The desert will lead you to your heart where I will speak."[6]

—*Paraphrase of Hosea 2:14*

There was a time she grudgingly called the "forty years in the desert." It was the mundane struggle with finances and work, with her family and friends, and with a body that wasn't in shape. It was easy to be numb (or want to be).

She had lost herself somewhere in the shuffle. What if this was how she would always feel? She always seemed to have more bills than paychecks. The kids were so demanding. On good days, her house looked like an explosion. It's not at all what she hoped it would be. Those thoughts swirled in her head as she got ready for bed.

She couldn't sleep. She was restless and agitated. She turned on her light and decided not to check her phone. Instead, she started reading her Bible. She remembered her comment about the "forty years" and decided to read about the people who had wandered in the desert. She flipped through the massive study Bible and found Psalm 78: "They forgot God's deeds as well as the wondrous works he showed them" (v. 11).

The people weren't thankful for what God had given them. They had been brought out of Egypt in a miraculous way, led safely, given daily bread, and still they complained. Was that what she had been doing?

She thought about her complaints. After reflecting, she started to realize her daily commute was beautiful and she had a comfortable place to sleep. She realized she had spent more time on texts than on her family. All of a sudden it wasn't her day that was meaningless, but her complaints. The "desert" was where she needed to be to realize how much she was missing.

And she found herself praying that she would be able to see her life in gratitude. God had helped her open her eyes to everything she was missing. She felt tired from the late night, but as her eyes closed, she couldn't help but think about the next day and how differently she would live. Maybe forty years would not be enough.

Prayer: Providing God, open my eyes to the wonders and miracles in my daily life. When I am distracted by work and finances, friends and family, and all the stresses of each day, bring me back to your marvelous works. In Christ, I pray. Amen.

Rev. Dr. Kristin D. Longenecker Hansen

Courage

According to Brené Brown, "The root of the word *courage* is cor, the Latin word for *heart*. In one of its earliest forms, the word *courage* meant "to speak one's mind by telling all one's heart." "Courage is a heart word," she says. So, "be brave. Love hard."[1]

Courage is contextual, and it is relational. It is what we need to be brave, try new things, and lead with boldness. Courage helps us do what we know we are called to do, even in the face of fear.

Too often for women, merely being present requires great courage. All around us every day, women boldly, bravely, and courageously break glass ceilings. We find the courage to live with this boldness by looking to the mothers of our faith, such as Joan of Arc, Harriet Tubman, Sally Ride, Aretha Franklin, Sandra Day O'Connor, or Mother Teresa.

While these extraordinary women inspire us through their courage, we also find courage in the midst of the ordinary. Sometimes, it begins with the act of getting out of bed in the morning and putting one foot in front of the other. Other times, our courage comes from deep within as we rely on the strength we draw from sisters around us as we act and speak bravely.

As women especially, we understand our presence can be considered a threat to those who project their own insecurities or fear of change onto us. We stand up against the status quo when we dare to be exactly who God created us to be. We must refuse to let anyone hold us down, to let the world take from us our strength and vulnerability, our convictions and dignity, our love and our honor. May the devotions that follow inspire you to be courageous in your daily life.

Indeed, may we have courage as we seek to be brave—and to love hard, together.

"I give you a new commandment: Love each other. Just as I have loved you, so you also must love each other. This is how everyone will know that you are my disciples, when you love each other."

—*John 13:34-35*

Courage and love go hand in hand. As do courage and fear. Courage is the ability to do something, to face something, to try something when afraid. Courage is the strength to endure pain or grief. Courage comes out of a great love that begins with Jesus Christ.

One of the biggest fears in life is trying something new or different. Fear overtakes courage when it begins to dictate life. With the love of God through Jesus Christ, courage can push fear to the back burner. Then the love of God dictates life. It is the love of God that says meet the neighbor. It is the love of God that says I am enough. It is the love of God that says try something new, it is good. It is the love of God that says fear will not win.

In this passage, Jesus and his disciples have come together for what would be their last supper. They share final moments of wisdom. They are full of love and fear as they find the courage to be together, to learn from one another, and to begin to understand life anew. The mystery of Jesus's death would not give way to fear. Courage would come out of their vulnerability as they talked openly about what was next in their lives. This new commandment is a powerful example of courage in the face of fear. It is a great act of courage to offer a self-sacrificing love. Jesus set the example himself. This great love is meant to be a uniting force rather than an act of division.

Whenever courage is needed, it is important to remember two key things. First, life-changing courage comes out of love rather than fear. Second, that love begins with Jesus Christ. Fear did not win on that first Easter, and it does not win today.

Prayer: God, I want the courage to hear your voice in this world. I want to stand up for what I know is right. I want not to be afraid, for the sake of your gospel. May I always remember the love that grounds me comes from you and is the birthplace of this courage that I long for. Courage looks more like love and less like fear. Amen.

Rev. Catherine Christman

I would encourage women to know first that I don't believe that
anyone is born with courage. I think you develop it. And life's
inventions can help you or discourage you to develop courage. . . .
I think you develop it in the same way you develop muscles.[2]

—*Maya Angelou*

A pirouette is when a ballet dancer spins around on one leg. It may seem effortless, but in fact, it's hard to master and takes a lot of training and focus to do it well. I can remember the systemic method my teacher used to try to get our muscles to remember the steps: first we did the arms, then we did the leg positions with the arms, and then we moved those together fluidly, all before ever taking a spin.

When it came time to finally let loose and spin, it was with great over-enthusiasm that we each went a quarter turn. I wanted to fly around and around and around like I saw principal dancers do onstage. Fortunately, we didn't stay at a quarter turn for long. In a matter of moments, we moved up past half and three-quarter turns, to full turns, and then one and a half turns.

Suddenly, it wasn't easy anymore. My classmates were flying around with ease and I was hitting my heels too soon, facing the wrong direction, flailing and falling over. My muscles weren't able to keep up with my spinning ambitions. It took weeks of extra practice, hours alone without recognition, congratulations, or outside encouragement. I needed to practice the basics over and over again to find how to embody it myself.

The most courageous people I know rarely have any idea how courageous they are because they have been practicing courage for so long; it is embodied in who they are. I have no way to fathom what work went in to their becoming courageous, but I do know that they started out learning the same way as I did—hitting their heels too soon, facing the wrong direction, flailing and falling, and trying again.

To be courageous people, we must practice the steps of courage, build the muscles of courage, and repeat. It means we must choose to be courageous in the little things so that when the time comes, we can step into having courage for the big things.

Prayer: Great Spirit, open my eyes to see the opportunities to be courageous that are all around. Give me the strength for today, and when I fall, give me the confidence to know that I am growing so that I may give it another spin when the challenges present themselves again tomorrow. Amen.

Rev. Sarah Karber

The king of Egypt spoke to two Hebrew midwives named
Shiphrah and Puah: "When you are helping the Hebrew women
give birth and you see the baby being born, if it's a boy, kill him
. . ." Now the two midwives respected God so they didn't obey the
Egyptian king's order. Instead, they let the baby boys live.

—*Exodus 1:15-17*

Very few times in history or myth have midwives been on center stage, but here, in the book of Exodus, their courage becomes legendary. Shiphrah and Puah are brought before the king of all Egypt, which in and of itself must have been at least unnerving. His instructions to them indicate that the meeting was terrifying: two small women before a powerful, unstable, genocidal man. He wants them to kill for him—to kill babies for him. We don't know how they responded in the moment. But we do know that they had courage. Courage to disobey authority.

In some ways, the courage to disobey authority is lacking in those of us with privilege. Authority protects our privilege. Authority rewards me for being white and performing my gender in a nonthreatening way. If I were to courageously take a stand against authority, what privilege I have would be in jeopardy. But the thing is, sometimes authority is unstable and violent. The rewards I get with my privilege come at a heavy price. White pastors like me might find saying that "black lives matter" from the pulpit may get us fired. But two centuries of white churches refusing to speak out about racism has allowed the church's prophetic voice to rot. Maybe you have found speaking out against authority to be dangerous as well. We look away from sexual harassment in the workplace, for instance, trying not to draw attention to ourselves. And yet, look at the sea change that has happened since some people have begun to speak out, regardless of the risk.

Shiphrah and Puah didn't care about privilege. They didn't care about authority. They cared about God. And so they courageously worked with

God to bring life into the world. I wonder what it would look like if I embodied courage like theirs. What would it look like for you? What privileges do you need to risk? What authorities do you need to disobey?

Prayer: Spirit, breathe life into me—strong, courageous life, to help me stand up to authority and live into your vision of justice and peace. Amen.

Rev. Shannon E. Sullivan

⌒ A Prayer for a Difficult Meeting ⌒

Lord, as I prepare for this upcoming meeting that is fraught with tension, I invite you to go before us into the room. I seek for you to open our ears for listening, to give us wisdom in speaking, and to break hearts open so we can follow your will in the actions we take. Amen.

Rev. Michelle R. Bodle

⌒ A Prayer for the Courage ⌒
to Speak Out Against Misconduct

It isn't right. I know it, God, and I know others know it. You know it. But the risks of naming this—racism, sexism, homophobia, harassment, assault, fraud, corruption, abuse of power—are many, and great.

I need this job. I need this community. I don't think I can do this on my own. What if no one believes me? Or they believe me, but still do nothing? What if I step out on this limb, and it breaks?

You, God, are the defender of the innocent, vindicator of the righteous. You promise that those who hunger and thirst for justice will be satisfied, that those who are persecuted for integrity's sake are blessed.

Bless me, then, O God: show me I am not alone, that you are with me. Steady my voice and strengthen my will; center my heart and still my trembling, so that I may bear witness to the truth, and the truth may set all of us free. Amen.

Rev. Kerry L. Greenhill

But the LORD wasn't in the wind. After the wind, there was an
earthquake. But the LORD wasn't in the earthquake. After the
earthquake, there was a fire. But the LORD wasn't in the fire.
After the fire, there was a sound. Thin. Quiet.

—1 Kings 19:11b-12.

This was my Mount Everest: a room full of strangers in a new city across the country from everyone and everything I ever knew. When I decided to make the move to graduate school, it seemed so adventurous, even romantic. But the reality was scary.

I was scared I had made the wrong choice. Scared I would fail.

But then at orientation, one of the professors called all of us new students—including me—"brave" for starting this journey. Brave was the last thing I felt. Two years of planning and preparing to get to this point, and still I was paralyzed by my own insecurity. Instead of a confident twenty-something young woman, I felt like a frightened little girl on her first day of kindergarten.

Then the professor repeated those words. Again, she said we were brave. That time, the words seeped into my very soul. And I started to believe. It wasn't an overwhelming flood, but more like a small pebble dropped on a long, winding gravel road. I started to believe I belonged there and that I was brave. Her words gave me assurance.

Sometimes courage isn't about big, bold moments but about those small, daily reminders that as you are brave and can do what scares you.

Perhaps that's just how God works sometimes. Elijah experienced God, not as howling wind, fire, or earthquake but rather thin, quiet.

Do you feel this assurance within you? I believe it's there. I hope you listen to it and look for God's hand that's extended out toward you.

Prayer: Holy Spirit, guide me to listen to your quiet voice over all other loud distractions and detractions. Assure me of your presence when I am scared. Remind me that I can do what scares me because you are here with me. Amen.

Rev. Katie Black

I hope, LORD. My whole being hopes, and I wait for God's prom-
ise. My whole being waits for my Lord—more than the night
watch waits for the morning; yes, more than the night watch
waits for the morning!

—*Psalm 130:5-6*

Several years ago, I joined Helen and her twelve-year-old son in a hospital waiting room. The doctor had just delivered shocking and almost unbearable news: the twelve-year-old would need a heart transplant if he were to live.

Despite what medical shows might have us believe, perfect hearts don't come along every day. Several months passed without news. A few times a week, I would sit with them as they waited. It felt like a pitiful offering on my part, but it was all I had to give.

During one of those visits, Helen shared, "It isn't the daytime which gets to me. It is the arrival of night. Doctors go home. Nurses are tired. People are sleeping. It's in those moments of quiet I feel the most afraid. So, I sit here and I watch over my son as he sleeps. I praise God for another day and for the promise of better days ahead. And then with my whole being, I wait for the morning light."

The waiting place. Perhaps you know it. Maybe you weren't waiting on a heart, but no doubt your time of waiting was also filled with anxiety and uncertainty. Anyone who stays in this place too long is likely to come undone.

What would it look like, instead, to choose hope over despair in our time of waiting? Could there be anything more courageous than to wait like Helen and the psalmist, with our whole beings, for God's light to come? Perhaps it is in these dark moments, when all we have left are God's promises, that faith can blossom.

While we cannot control what challenges tomorrow will bring, we can choose how we respond to them. Be bold. Be brave. Be confident that the darkness never has the last word. Wait on the Lord!

Prayer: God of waiting, I am thankful that wherever we may find ourselves, you are already there. Give me courage to wait on you with my entire being and trust that whatever else the dawning light may bring, it will also bring a word of hope from you. Amen.

Rev. Leslie Stephens

And sometimes, just showing up, burial spices in hand, is all it takes to witness a miracle.[3]

—*Rachel Held Evans*

As I ran from one side of the hospital to the other that day, all I could think about was how scared I was, not knowing what to say or do. I was only interning as a hospital chaplain. What could I offer to these parents whose nine-year-old son died on the way to the hospital?

I prayed for courage as my supervisor and I comforted the family, anointed the body, and spoke words that could have only been God-given in that moment. By the grace of God, the family was grateful, even in the midst of their sadness. I learned a powerful truth that day: God will use our very presence as a means of grace to others, even in the midst of our fears and anxieties, to work miracles.

Life is full of painful moments in which we are called upon to show up and, by our very being, offer comfort and healing. In those times, we must step up to the plate, whether or not we feel prepared. "Do not be afraid," Scripture tells us over and over again. Do not be afraid that you will not have the right words or actions to offer. Do not be afraid that you will fail or embarrass yourself. Do not be afraid because God will work through you.

One of the most important things we must remember as women in leadership is that the courage to walk into the room and show up is a bold act. When you are afraid, remember to take heart and place your words, your actions, and your very being into God's hands.

On that first Easter morning, the women set out to perform the heart-wrenching task of washing and anointing the body of their beloved Jesus. Heartbroken, unsure if they could even roll away the stone, afraid of what they would find, still they went. With great courage, they showed up, even as others cowered away in an upper room. They gathered their courage, showed up with nothing but burial spices in hand, and there they witnessed a miracle.

What miracle might you witness today if you choose courage over fear?

Prayer: Ever-present God, help me set aside my fears and anxieties in holy and difficult moments. Help me imagine what miracles await me and how You will use me when I dare to show up, prepared to carry out your work. Amen.

Rev. Jill Howard

A Prayer When Experiencing a Panic Attack

I am in pain.

I feel scared to the point I want to jump out of my skin and run away. Or maybe crawl under the covers and make myself as small as possible. I pray for the courage to face this fear.

With strength, I turn inside to find the pain and explain it to you. Hear me—that I may finally feel that I am fully seen and known. All of my pain and all of my beauty brought to light. Great Comforter, bathe my suffering in your love and compassion. Let me feel comfort as lush as a rain forest, freedom that makes my heart soar high into the clouds, and peace as deep as the oceans. Amen.

Rev. Julia Singleton

A Prayer at the Time of Burnout

God of mercy, I confess I feel like I am bereft of sinew, a bag of dry bones, and my spirit in ashes. I have tried to take it all on myself. I have failed to seek sustenance. Give me courage to seek help. Help me find a moment of Sabbath today, breathe into me and revive these bones. Help me trust that you will walk with me though this land. Amen.

Rev. Sarah Karber

We can choose courage or we can choose comfort, but we can't have both. Not at the same time.[4]

—*Brené Brown*

I found myself in the midst of a difficult work situation where I was faced with a choice: be a bold and courageous leader or keep my head down and be comfortable. Either option would have been acceptable, given the circumstances, but I felt God nudging me toward the courageous one.

It's hard to have courage when you're faced with seemingly impossible odds. In this case, I knew courageous leadership would make some people angry but would ultimately do the most good. I also knew choosing comfort would lead to personal dissonance, making me unhappy and unable to live out my role at work. After some prayer and reflection, I knew choosing courageous leadership would be difficult but would be the right choice.

In order to be courageous, you have to know yourself and build a community of people who can remind you to be courageous, even when things get difficult. Choosing courage is uncomfortable. As human beings, we're naturally predisposed to seek what is comfortable. Choosing courage is difficult, but you are a gifted, capable, and beloved child of God, who is able to do difficult things.

Sometimes, all we need is the reminder that God loves us and invites us to courageously change the world. So, beloved child of God, how is God calling you to be courageous today? What choices do you need to make? What comforts do you need to let go of? Who are the people who will support you in your courageous decisions?

Prayer: Holy God, give me the strength and the courage I need. Grant me peace in the midst of difficulty and strength to continue the good work you have asked of me. In the name of our Savior, Jesus Christ. Amen.

Rev. Lorrin M. Radzik

When Jesus had been baptized, just as he came up from the water, suddenly the heavens were opened to him and he saw the Spirit of God descending like a dove and alighting on him. And a voice from heaven said, "This is my Son, the Beloved, with whom I am well pleased."

—*Matthew 3:16-17 (NRSV)*

I was seven months old, and my mother was pacing nervously in the hospital, fearfully wondering what was yet to come. I, her youngest daughter, had been diagnosed with meningitis, and the doctors didn't have any good news for her. They weren't sure I would make it, and if I did, would I be deaf? have physical impairments? something else? It wasn't looking good.

As all of her body shook with fear, she took a step of courage she didn't know she had. That day in the hospital, she offered me to God through baptism. "Please, O God, as I turn Jen's life over to you, may you care for and heal her," she prayed. "If you spare her life, I promise we will set her aside for great things. We offer her to you, that she might grow to love and to serve you all her days." For all of my life, my mother promised she would help me draw near to God. Whatever that might look like, in life or in death: she courageously trusted God to care for me.

In the moment of Jesus's baptism, God's only son, Jesus, was entrusted to us in a similar way. "This is my Son, the Beloved, with whom I am well pleased," God's voice declared from the heavens.

I imagine the witnesses of this moment wondering what that might mean and what the life of this newly baptized Son of God might come to be. I imagine they were watching, prayerful, as they waited for whatever was yet to come of Jesus's life.

In many ways, that's what happened in the hospital room at my own baptism too. With family gathered near, watching, waiting, and making promises on my behalf, they found themselves uncertain and afraid.

Decades later, we are grateful there are no negative long-term effects of this illness that came so close to taking my life. Yet God's promise offered in the moment of our baptism remains:

"This is my [child], the Beloved, with whom I am well pleased."

In our baptism, we also inherit this title alongside the opportunity to courageously follow Christ with all that we say and do.

Prayer: Holy and loving God, help me turn my life over to you, that I might love and serve you with all of my days. Be with me in each breath I take and every moment that passes. May I find strength and courage in your presence as I breathe in your spirit and prepare to face the impossible. Amen.

Rev. Jen Tyler

Now, I have been loyal to you. So pledge to me by the LORD that
you in turn will deal loyally with my family. Give me a sign
of good faith. Spare the lives of my father, mother, brothers, and
sisters, along with everything they own. Rescue us from death.

—*Joshua 2:12-13*

Joshua's first act as leader of the Israelites after the death of Moses is to send two spies into the Promised Land, targeting Jericho. The spies meet Rahab, a prostitute who must provide for her extended family. Rahab unapologetically and assertively strikes a deal with the spies: I will help you take Jericho if you spare my family.

Rahab's story, from beginning to end, is one of courage as she engages in risky business to provide for her family. She hides the Israelite spies as she diverts the king and his military, and she plots the spies' escape to the traditional outlaw refuge—the hills. This trickster serves as a prophet, sharing God's deliverance of the Promised Land to God's people. She is also a hero, serving as a change agent who rose to the occasion of God's call to stand up to both the authorities of Jericho and the spies. In doing so, she changes the history of her family and of a nation.

This is a story about rising up, the marginalized changing the course of their history, and of one woman who had the courage and audacity to do something about the injustices of her system. "Rahab the prostitute," her identifier through the Hebrew Bible and the New Testament, was the first Canaanite convert. She is listed in Jesus's family tree in Matthew and is lifted up as faithful and righteous in the books of James and Hebrews. She clearly made an impact on Jewish and Christian history by stepping up and out from where she lived—on the edge of town, with the stigma of her job attached—to do what God called her to do.

Living courageously is a faithful act. In what ways are you called to step up and out from stigmas to do what God is calling you to do?

Prayer: Audacious God, your faith in me is wondrous. Grant me strength, so I may live courageously and audaciously like Rahab, stepping up to serve as a change agent in both easy and challenging times. May I always stand up for those who are marginalized and have no voice. Grant me the audacity to move mountains in the face of power, even when I am shaky and afraid. Amen.

Rev. Melissa Engel

A Prayer When a Partner Is Not Able to Be Supportive

Merciful God, I thank you for the support that my partner has given me in the past. I was blessed to have someone to cry with me, celebrate with me, and rant with me. I grieve that this is not what is happening now in my need. I am angry and I am disappointed.

I ask for your compassion to fall upon my partner, that whatever difficulties my partner is facing are nothing compared to your power.

Help me find others to help lift me up as I walk through this hard time. Send me those who can hear my fears and frustrations, whose words will cut through the sorrows and the sufferings. May they be a balm to my wounded soul. And may I always rely on you, my Creator and Perfecter, that in everything, I remember to lean on your strength and trust in your kindness. Amen.

Rev. Heather Dorr

A Prayer for Daily Busyness

Holy God, uncertainty makes me feel like the ground is shifting and balance is beyond my reach. This day calls for grace upon grace. Grace that heals. Grace that binds us together. Grace that reminds us that we cannot do life alone. Grace that connects and reconnects your diverse and beautiful people.

Breathe into my weary soul, reviving me from doubt and fear. Enable me to catch on, catch up, and move forward. Walk near, for I am still searching for a firm foundation. Amen.

Rev. Blair Tolbert

"Be strong and courageous," David said to his son Solomon.
"Get to work. Don't be afraid or discouraged, because the LORD
God, my God, is with you. He'll neither let you down nor leave
you before all the work for the service of the LORD's temple is
done."

—*1 Chronicles 28:20*

David is not known in Scripture for his parenting ability, but his words to his son Solomon in this passage are ones parents might want to echo. He is encouraging, challenging, and pushing Solomon to do what David knows is good for him, good for the world, good in the long run. Get to work. Don't be afraid, just do it. It is going to be OK.

My six-year-old daughter recently tried out for her school play. The stakes were not high, as everyone who signed up got a part, and the play was only open to early elementary students. To her, however, the play was a very big deal.

The year before, my expressive, creative, extroverted daughter had been too nervous to speak in front of an audience. She was unsure and didn't see herself the way her father and I do—as a born leader and perfect candidate for theatrics. We threw the sign-up sheet in the garbage and signed her up for swim lessons instead. When the play came up this year, she thought about it for all of two minutes before declaring that she wanted to go for it. Still, she was nervous. I know this because she told me every evening for weeks.

The day of auditions, she was apprehensive and quieter than normal. I brought her to school, where she clung to my side. After checking in, she asked if I could stay for a bit. We walked in together, where she saw two of her classmates. She immediately abandoned me, laughing, and ran to them. "Jacob! Haley!" and sat down next to them, animated and excited. As soon as she realized she wasn't alone, that she had friends in the room, she had the courage she needed to do the work.

Whether we are leading children through a life of risk-taking, leading a community in pursuit of justice, or leading ourselves to speak our truth, God is with us. God shows up in the midst of our fears, our second-guesses, and our reluctance. *Get to work*, God says to us. *Do what you need to do. I'm right here next to you. You are not alone. It will be OK.*

Prayer: God, You are the God of David, of Solomon, of me. May I remember you are with me all the days of my life. As we face our fears and tackle our challenges, grant us courage and strength to do our work. May your presence amplify our voices and magnify our confidence. Amen.

Rev. Brooke Heerwald Steiner

*I finally concluded that all failure was from a wobbling will
rather than a wobbling wheel.*[5]

—*Frances Willard*

I lived in Evanston, Illinois, for three years and was introduced to a local heroine while there—Frances Willard, a Methodist American educator, reformer, and women's suffragist. Though I may not share her complete commitment to temperance, I continue to be inspired by her story.

Frances worked tirelessly in the 1800s to advocate for women who were affected by the violence and poverty that arose from their spouses' alcohol addiction. She believed women and men should lead side by side in the home, the church, society, and political reform. Frances was a larger-than-life character, never seeming to be deterred from her commitment to work for the common good, and she was always—always—moving. She is most famous for traveling by bike to be sure she could reach the most people with her message in as little time as possible.

Even these change agents that remind us of what courage is are human, and no doubt they experienced their own failure of nerve. Frances reflects, "That which caused the many failures I had in learning the bicycle had caused me failures in life; namely a certain fearful looking for of judgment; . . . uncertainty of everything about me; an underlying doubt—at once, however, matched and overcome by the determination not to give in to it."[6]

I believe this determination arises from the unswerving belief in the constant nature of God's presence. The prophet Ezekiel once spoke to an exiled people who believed that God's glory was always in the land and that God was not with them. Ezekiel shared a vision of chariots riding and a wheel within a wheel, saying, "When [the wheels] moved in any of the four directions, they moved without swerving" (Ezekiel 1:17). This vision was meant to reveal to them that God goes with God's people in exile—that the presence of God is always mobile, never tethered, and can always be sought and found.

If you're like me, you might be plagued with missed opportunities, memories of complicit silence and dreams deferred because of a lack of courage. When I have believed in that presence and power wholeheartedly, I have experienced renewed resolve to take on tough challenges, try new things, and risk my own privilege for those communities and causes that matter most.

What would you do today if you knew, without a doubt, that God's presence would follow you and fill every need wherever you go?

Prayer: Lord, may I approach today, and all days, with an unswerving faith in you. Amen.

Rev. Katie McKay Simpson

Then the prophet Miriam, Aaron's sister, took a tambourine in her hand. All the women followed her playing tambourines and dancing. Miriam sang the refrain back to them: Sing to the LORD, for an overflowing victory! Horse and rider he threw into the sea!

—*Exodus 15:20-21*

For many years I have learned leadership lessons from Moses, but to lead today, I need the wisdom of the prophet Miriam, the sister of Moses and Aaron. Scripture captures a key moment in her leadership of the people on their journey. They've just escaped Pharaoh's army and crossed through the waters, miraculously. People are probably still anxious about all they left behind as they fled Egypt, narrowly escaping death. This is now the moment when Miriam knows the people must pause to celebrate.

She leads the women in playing instruments and dancing. She sings praises for God's work to save the people fleeing captivity. She knows in that moment the people must stop to express gratitude and to name the way God has been at work in their midst.

As a leader, I don't naturally stop to celebrate the progress we've made. I'm often focused on how far we have to go and what our next steps are. But, when the journey is long and arduous, it is vital that we pause regularly to notice how God has been at work, in order to bravely move through uncertainty.

When we notice God at work, through small or big ways, the prophet Miriam can remind us that this is cause for celebration. My hope is that even when we're scared about what might come in the next part of our journey, we can take up our instruments and lead people in praising God for the miraculous moments along the way.

Prayer: I lift my voice in praise to you, God. I have come so far, though there is still a long way to go until I see your vision for my life and this world fully realized. Thank you for all the ways you are at work in my life and my community. Help me be brave enough to set down my "to do" for the next step, to stop and notice your work in our midst, and then to praise you for that work. Amen.

Rev. Sarah Harrison-McQueen

⌒ A Prayer for Fertility Treatment ⌒

God of creation, I come to you in the midst of this fertility treatment, grateful for the ways that you have been at work in my life. Guide the work of my doctors, be with my care team, and protect me during this treatment. O God, you know the desires of my heart and the steps of my journey that have led to this place. Heal me in mind, soul, and body so that I might be a ready for the gift of creation within me. Grant me peace and trust in the days of waiting ahead, and strengthen me for all that comes next. In the name of Jesus, the Word made flesh. Amen.

Rev. Lorrin M. Radzik

⌒ A Prayer at the Time ⌒ of Premature Birth

God of our lives, there are moments for which there are no words. No words for the moment when my child has been separated from me because they have entered the world too soon. Through the beeping of the machines, the feeling of warm air flowing inside Isolettes, the sight of breast pumps expressing liquid gold, and the smell of hand soap, help me feel your presence.

Surround my baby and me and with your peace, and remind us that we are not alone and that we are loved unconditionally. I pray that this baby grows stronger each moment, and that doctors and nurses care for this baby as their own. Give me courage as I leave my baby each day and bravery to face the ups and downs.

You, O God, are my rock. I lean on you. Amen.

Rev. Kaleigh Corbett

*{Anna} was now an 84-year-old widow. She never left the
temple area but worshipped God with fasting and prayer night
and day. She approached at that very moment and began to
praise God and to speak about Jesus to everyone who was looking
forward to the redemption of Jerusalem.*

—*Luke 2:37-38*

Who are the women in your life who inspire you? What is it about them that inspires you?

There are many women who inspire me. I know some of these women personally, like my mother and my best friend. There are also women who inspire me who I have never met or know only from history: Maya Angelou, Rosa Parks, and Corrie ten Boom, as well as biblical women like Ruth and Anna, the prophet. There is a unifying thread in these women's lives that I find profoundly inspiring: they have chosen to live courageously on their own terms.

I have always loved Anna's story in particular. Her brief appearance in Scripture peaks my curiosity. It makes me ask questions like: How long has she been a widow? Does she have any living family members? What led her to devote her life to worshipping God around the clock in the temple? What do her friends and family think about her spending all of her time at the temple?

One can only imagine the whispers that accompany Anna when she walks into the room. And yet, that doesn't stop her. Anna lives life on her own terms. She is faithful to following God with all of her life. Anna's reward for being true to the person God created her to be is seeing Jesus in the flesh.

Especially as a woman in today's world, there are times when I feel boxed in to be, act, or look a certain way. I can be easily derailed by criticism, judgment, fear of failing, or many other things.

Anna's story, like the stories of so many other inspiring women, reminds us not to be afraid to live into God's call on our lives and to live courageously no matter what others may think. Anna was a unique creation of God. I am a unique creation of God. You are a unique creation of God. How can you live courageously into the unique person God created you to be?

Prayer: Creating God, thank you for the unique gifts and qualities you have poured into my life. May you give me the courage to live life faithfully, boldly, and courageously into the fullness of what you set before me. Amen.

Rev. Sara Nelson

God is within her, she will not fall.

—*Psalm 46:5 (NIV)*

I once heard a speech by a Navy SEAL admiral in which he said if you make your bed, you will have accomplished the first task of the day.[7] Well, I need him to back up a step. The first task of my day is getting out of bed.

Some days, just getting out of bed is the hardest thing I do: out of the safety of its warmth and protective covers. Getting out of bed means it's time to face the harsh realities of another day. It takes courage to get out of bed some days.

On those days, the very mundane task of getting out of bed, leaving the warmth and comfort of its shelter, may be the most laborious task of all.

Like on the day after my divorce, when I was really and truly a single mother of two kids.

Or the day after you find out a good friend has a life-changing disease.

Or the day you have to lead a meeting like a boss when you feel like a piece of gum stuck on someone's shoe.

It's then that the words of the psalmist come to mind. It isn't by our strength that we press on, but through God, who dwells within us. From the very depths of our soul, God encourages us to get up, to go, to keep pushing forward! I hear God's word: "Get out of bed, you can do it!"

Courage means so many things, but on the hardest and cruelest days of our lives, it is the capacity to throw off the warm blankets, put two feet on the cold floor, and get out of bed to face another day. It means knowing that whatever else we may face that day, we have accomplished this task. It means living with the assurance God's strength dwells deep within us, encouraging us to move forward.

May you draw on the same wellspring of strength and courage to face the day, to keep going, and to take one more step forward until at last you return to the safety and comfort of your warm shelter.

Prayer: Steadfast God, hold me close this day as I go forward from my sanctuary to meet the world. Be with me as I face the challenges of this day and carry me back to this place with peace. Amen.

Rev. Danyelle Trexler

Finally, be strong in the Lord and in the strength of his power. Put on the whole armor of God, so that you may be able to stand against the wiles of the devil. For our struggle is not against enemies of blood and flesh, but against the rulers, against the authorities, against the cosmic powers of this present darkness.

—Ephesians 6:10-12 (NRSV)

Courage is your head held high, shoulders squared off, eyes set and focused. It's consistency in the chaos more than a single choice. It's cultivated over time instead of by a spur-of-the-moment flash of boldness. Courage is practiced in a woman's posture.

The powers of the world have shrewdly defined how women are supposed to look, act, and generally be. And much to our chagrin, these messages have seeped into our very souls. Our bodies have been called too big and too small, our voices called too loud and too quiet, our wardrobes said to be too casual and too uptight, and our lives thought to be too family-focused or too ambitious. Finding voice, holding fast, charging forward, taking heart, stepping out, and developing a posture of courage in the midst of this messaging is a challenge.

We are often quick to assign the blame to an individual, like a particular man. Sometimes, we have blamed institutions like the church or corporate America. But in truth, the power we stand against, the one Paul spoke about, is greater than any person or institution. It's a systemic patriarchy that attacks us from every side with a flood of unachievable expectations.

If we are to stand with courage against the power of patriarchy, then we must practice our posture, beginning with putting on the clothing of God. Through this practiced discipline, we intentionally remind ourselves we are claimed and made whole through the waters of baptism, shielded by our shared calling to build up the kingdom in the world, clad in new identities as beloved children of God, and adorned with grace through our Savior Jesus Christ.

Prayer: God, you are bold. Make me bold. You are sure. Make me sure. You are courageous. Make me courageous. You are good. Make me good. You are full of grace. Mark me with your grace, mold me to be graceful, and make me to offer grace to all I meet. Amen.

Rev. Brandi Tevebaugh Horton

⌒ A Prayer Before Asking for a Raise ⌒

Empowering God, I know that my worth is not measured by my salary but comes from your unconditional love for me regardless of my station in life. But for many reasons, I believe it is time to ask for a raise, and I want to do this faithfully and well.

Grant me humility and courage in equal measure, to know I am no greater and no less than others. Help me see clearly how I contribute to my employer, where I can continue to grow, and how to keep blessing others through my work. Help me speak confidently, to respond thoughtfully, and to move forward graciously whatever the answer.

May I remain open to hearing the whispers of your Spirit as I seek to follow Jesus in my work no less than in the rest of my life. Amen.

Rev. Kerry L. Greenhill

⌒ A Prayer in the Midst of a Job Change ⌒

O God, in this moment, as I consider what a new job will mean, I pray for your guidance and your peace.

I lay before you my worries and my fears as I'm unsure about what this change will mean for my routine, my family, and my future. I turn over to you my grief as I end this chapter of my life and say good-bye to colleagues, projects, and plans. I pray that this change will bring new challenges that lead to transformation and new opportunities that lead to growth.

Grant me wisdom and grace, for myself and others, as I navigate this transition. May I forever keep your call on my life at the forefront of every decision I make, in work and in life. Amen.

Rev. Kristin Heiden

> *But Moses said to the people, "Do not be afraid, stand firm, and*
> *see the deliverance that the LORD will accomplish for you today;*
> *for the Egyptians whom you see today you shall never see again.*
> *The Lord will fight for you, and you have only to keep still."*
>
> *—Exodus 14:13-14 (NRSV)*

A t this point in the Exodus story, the people of God have accepted the divine invitation to participate in their own liberation. Although their journey toward liberation has only just begun, the people of God have already demonstrated that God inspires courage that takes many different forms. It comes under the heel of hopeless oppression, manifests in the guttural cry "how long, O Lord," and is present in the midst of the mystical horror of plagues and chaos. Courage manifests to stoke the fire of faith, and in the depths of the deadly night, it manifests in the hasty communal movement toward the unknown wilderness with tambourine clutched in hand.

In Exodus 14, the people have responded to God's invitation. They have become cocreators in their own liberation, and yet God's call to courage does not cease. In this passage, the community of God finds itself trapped at the edge of the Sea of Reeds while the Egyptian army bears down with fire and fury.

God calls people to a courage of another kind: the courage to wait. Of all the courageous ways God empowers people to act, this is perhaps one of the hardest to accept. It requires people to trust in the power of God in the face of the unthinkable.

In moments of terror, God invites people to choose a way of counterintuitive courage: Don't be afraid. Stand firm. Keep still. Far from a call to passive submission, this is a summons to the most radical courage people can muster in the face of a circumstance beyond their control. This invitation is for you as well.

In the face of the unthinkable, the unmanageable, and the seemingly unsurvivable, God invites us to a courage of another kind. Don't be afraid. Stand your ground. God has your back; the Lord will fight for you.

Prayer: God of liberation, help me be courageous as I face the circumstances of my day. Help me discern the action you call me toward, especially when it is a call to be still and let you fight for me. Help me trust that you will make a way when I see no way, and to face the future unafraid. Amen.

Rev. Colleen Hallagan Preuninger

Levi responded and said to Peter, "Peter, you have always been an angry person. Now I see you contending against the woman like the adversaries. But if the Savior made her worthy, who are you, then, to reject her? Surely the Savior's knowledge of her is trustworthy. That is why he loved her more than us. Rather, let us be ashamed."[8]

—*Gospel of Mary 10:7-11a*

The Gospel of Mary, believed to be written about Mary Magdalene and her journey with Christ, shares the insights Mary gained as a close confidante of Christ. She consoles the disciples after Jesus's death and shares the insights she gained during their time together. Based on what we read in the Gospels, she may have been the only woman in the room when the disciples gathered.

Despite the fact that the male disciples would have traveled with her and would have seen, firsthand, the close relationship she had with Jesus, some of the disciples still question her authority.

Jesus, according to this Gospel, told Mary some things he didn't tell anyone else. Andrew and Peter are astonished. Peter actually says: "Did he really speak with a woman without our knowing about it?"[9] Mary responds like many of us would: she weeps. She demands to know why Peter would suggest she is lying. In this room full of men, she allows her frustration to show. Levi speaks up for her, being her advocate and ally.

Can you imagine being Mary, sharing experiences, knowledge, and ideas, only to be met with such a response?

I can, and I'm guessing you can as well. If you've ever been the only woman in the room, you've been there. If you've ever had men interrupt you or re-explain what you've just said, you've been there. If you've watched others take credit for your work, you've been there.

There are days when simply showing up takes a tremendous amount of courage. There are moments when speaking our truth is the most courageous act we can imagine. We can courageously allow our pain and frustration to show, too, as Mary did. And when we're tired, exhausted, or frustrated, we can even allow an advocate or ally to take up our cause alongside us.

Prayer: Holy One, you have entrusted us with experiences and expertise. Give me the courage to face situations and spaces where I will be questioned, chastised, and ignored. Help me remember that you entrusted a woman with the most holy tasks of all: bearing your Son into the world and declaring his resurrection. I, too, am worthy of your good news. Amen.

Rev. J. Paige Boyer

*Know this, my dear brothers and sisters: everyone should be quick
to listen, slow to speak, and slow to grow angry.*

—James 1:19

One of the most difficult parts of leading comes when it is time for hard conversations. As a leader, you will inevitably ruffle feathers, step on toes, and even make mistakes. When those things occur, the hard conversations begin. I have tried to avoid them, thinking the issue will just go away on its own. I have tried to pass them off to other people, falsely believing I am just good at delegating and don't need to deal directly with the issue. I have tried to settle the problem over e-mail and even more broadly in an organization-wide newsletter. With each attempt, however, the problem seems to grow and tension continues to build.

So, what must I do? Have the hard conversation with the courage to face what is coming. The courageous act does not end with initiating the conversation, although it is a beginning. No, the bulk of the courage must come in the midst of the conversation. Will I be willing to listen without formulating my rebuttal? Will I be able to empathize instead of judging? Will I choose my words carefully and allow them to be framed with grace and compassion instead of anger and ego? And when a legitimate concern is expressed, will I have the strength to admit fault and ask for forgiveness?

The courage and strength of a leader is shown most clearly not in moments of success, but in moments of challenge. While it is important to remain true to our convictions, to stay firm in our foundations, we must face the difficult conversations in a way that unites instead of divides, allowing space for compassion and reconciliation. May we have the courage to engage in the hard conversations with grace and peace as our guide.

Prayer: O Lord, I give thanks for the call you have placed on my life, and I pray for your strength and guidance as I seek to live into my role as a leader at

139

work, at home, and in the life of faith. I am grateful for every moment, successes and failures. When the challenges arise, I pray you will grant me courage to maintain this faith-filled leadership. Help me live into these words of James, that I may be quick to listen, slow to speak, and slow to grow angry in every conversation so that your love and grace may be shared even in the difficult conversations. Amen.

Rev. Kristin Heiden

∼ A Prayer for Wisdom When ∼
Considering Leaving a Spouse

My God, my God: I am feeling forsaken.[10] My dreams for my life are faded and ragged, but I've been holding on to them anyway. Holding out hope that my partner will be the person I married . . . or perhaps the person I had hoped I had married. But while I have held out hope, nothing has gotten better; nothing has changed. Except I have changed. I am not myself. My bones are out of joint, my heart feels melted within me. Do not be far off. Guide me. Give me wisdom to live into my dreams again, even if they are new dreams. Even if they are difficult. Even if they are dreams to be lived into without my spouse. Amen.

Rev. Shannon E. Sullivan

∼ A Prayer for the Day ∼
of Your Divorce Hearing

Holy God, wrap me in your peace as I take this final step toward freedom from this person who is no longer a partner in life. Give me courage and strength to go through this day with dignity, self-respect, and the knowledge I am worthy of more. Remind me, O God, I am your beloved daughter! And in the course of time, help me forgive, heal, and move forward with my life so I may experience the gift of joy anew. Amen.

Rev. Danyelle Trexler

Don't fear, because I am with you; don't be afraid, for I am your God. I will strengthen you, I will surely help you; I will hold you with my righteous strong hand.

—*Isaiah 41:10*

Often when I think of courage, I think of those great historical moments, those famous images and stories, when someone did what was "right" even at great risk to her reputation, her livelihood, or her life. I think of Rosa Parks sitting down on that bus, of Harriet Tubman escaping slavery and then going back into danger to rescue others, or of Malala Yousafzai who dared to attend school and advocate for girls' right to education.

These are inspiring acts of courage that model for me what is possible for any of us to do, even in the face of great fear and great risk. They remind me that any of us can gather our God-given strength and do scary things to make a difference in the world. Rosa, Harriet, and Malala were and are ordinary women of faith who dared to do extraordinary things, to do the "right" thing no matter what.

But most days, courage doesn't look so extraordinary in my life. My life is rarely on the line, and my moments of courage will likely go unnoticed by others. For me, courage comes in those everyday experiences when I have a choice to be my true self in a world that doesn't always welcome that, to face life's challenges head-on rather than running from them, to speak up about what I know to be true and right and just. As a hospital chaplain, courage often looks like sitting in a room with a grieving family begging to know why God would take their loved one when I have no easy answers for them and would rather run away from that room of despair. Or it looks like speaking up in conversation with friends or coworkers when I hear them talking from places of white privilege. Or the courage comes when I can admit my mistakes and apologize to someone I have wronged.

This isn't the courage that makes the history books, but it's what courage looks like for many of us every day when we have choices before us asking us to take the courageous path. May we be mindful of each of those opportunities and feel the strength of the Spirit offering us courage.

Prayer: Holy God, fill me with the assurance that I am strengthened and held by you. May that strength allow me to live courageously every day, in both the ordinary and extraordinary moments. Amen.

Rev. Dr. Christina L. Wright

I've commanded you to be brave and strong, haven't I? Don't be alarmed or terrified, because the LORD your God is with you wherever you go.

—Joshua 1:9

God called Joshua to lead the Israelites into the Promised Land after Moses's death. I imagine Joshua felt overwhelmed. He had lost his friend and mentor. In the midst of his and the Israelites' grief, God called him into a new role as leader of a people who had wandered the desert and faced difficult moments during the Exodus. Taking them to the Promised Land may have been bittersweet and certainly would not have been an easy task. God meets Joshua in the midst of his grief, fear, and uncertainty and offers words wrapped in great care and grace. Have courage, Joshua! From that courage, remember: I am with you wherever you go.

In my own life, I remember feeling overwhelmed at the start of my first pastorate. There were moments I was filled with doubt, moments I wanted to give up, and moments I felt unsure of why God called me to walk alongside people in pain. God's grace would gently meet me in those moments to give me courage—usually through other people. I would frequently receive a phone call or note from friends reminding me that I was indeed doing what God had called me to do. My very first Sunday school teacher always seemed to know when I needed to be reminded of God's presence with me and would drop a note in the mail filled with words that would speak to my uncertainty, reminding me to continue to be brave and strong no matter how overwhelming the journey felt. Her words of grace helped me to feel and see that God was with me, wherever I went.

Joshua wasn't the first or last to be asked to do what seemed impossible. Like Joshua, when God calls us, God will sustain us and offer us words of courage along the way. May you be so bold as to receive that courage and live into your God-given call, remembering that the Lord your God is with you wherever you go.

Prayer: Gracious God, give me bravery and strength. In moments of doubt and when I feel overwhelmed by the weight of your call, meet me with your grace. Offer me reminders that no matter where I go you are with ne. Amen.

Rev. Lauren A. Godwin

⌒ A Prayer for Waiting in a Time ⌒
of Medical Uncertainty

Holy One who lights my way, in my uncertainty, be my guide, my comfort, and my strength.

As I await answers from my medical team, I call upon you for hope and peace and ask that you bless those who care for me with wisdom, compassion, and skill for this work to which you have called them.

Ease any fear or anxiety that burdens my heart and mind and help me feel your presence with me here and now. Bless me that I may trust you no matter the outcome. Amen.

Rev. Jennifer Zeigler Medley

Resistance

There is a fairly common saying that we don't know who discovered water, but it certainly wasn't a fish. It is extremely difficult to see the water we're swimming in—it surrounds us and has always been there. We don't examine it critically; it's just what's around us. Resistance is about doing just that—critically examining everything we are "swimming" in. Moreover, resistance is about not just accepting that it's the way it has to be, but rather seeing it for what it is and knowing we can do something about it.

Our culture is all around us. Culture feels different to different people and is different in different places. There are many, many wonderful things about different cultures—food, art, music, and religion are all cultural. So, too, are things like social expectations, government, and schools. We can and must examine the cultures we swim in if we are to resist those things in our cultures that are not a reflection of the wondrous, just, and loving Creator God.

When we look at the culture in the United States critically, we are aware of many of our social ills. We see poverty, racism, classism, sexism, ageism, sizeism, heterosexism, and transphobia. We see inequality between people, all of whom are loved deeply by God. We see how capitalism has a foothold in places like our education and health-care systems. We see people suffering. And we hear voices telling us that this is just the way things are or that this is all good. We receive messages daily about how we shouldn't upset things too much, how we should accept and be grateful for what we have. As women especially, we are told no one will listen to us if we try to change things, and that we are being idealistic or emotional to think that we should.

Resistance is knowing these voices are lying. Resistance is seeing the

147

positive and negative aspects of the cultures we swim in and feeling God moving within us to work for change. After all, we follow Jesus Christ who entered this world to completely turn it upside down and bring forth the kin-dom[1] of God where all the wrongs will be made right.

The devotions that follow will sustain you, challenge you, and comfort you in your journey of resistance. Here you will find Scriptures, insights, and prayers to help you call out injustice where you see it, drown out the lies, and live an active life in pursuit of truth. We hope these devotions bless you as you discover the water, including its pollutants, and work relentlessly to be a force to purify it with the love, justice, and peace of God.

*Don't be conformed to the patterns of this world, but be trans-
formed by the renewing of your minds so that you can figure out
what God's will is—what is good and pleasing and mature.*

—Romans 12:2

R esistance begins in the mind.

As a part of my devotional life, I attend a yoga class led by a deeply wise and discerning woman. As she guides us in our practice, she encourages us to cultivate the garden of our mind. Each class she prompts us to turn our attention to our thoughts, encouraging us to consider whether the thoughts we are cultivating serve our goals of spiritual health and wholeness; I am always surprised to discover the remnants of old fears, frameworks, and expectations growing in my mind.

Practicing yoga in a group has always been a challenge for me; it has required that I deconstruct long-standing frameworks of cultural expectations of women's bodies—how they should look and where they are welcome. The awareness this practice cultivates offers the space to identify and deconstruct harmful thoughts that do not serve the purposes of health and wholeness. It is only when I become aware of what is growing in my mind that I can begin to cultivate a different inner environment to shape my thoughts and actions.

How are you cultivating the garden of your mind? What thoughts and attitudes are growing there?

The apostle Paul argued for the importance of cultivating the garden of the mind in his letter to the Romans. He knew that the only way to resist unhealthy and unjust systems was by first cultivating the inner world of the mind. For Paul, this meant cultivating a devotional life that allows the mind of Christ to continually renew and transform the minds of Christ followers.

Paul knew that the first (and most insidious) obstacle in living a life that

149

embodies the countercultural and subversive life of Jesus is the deconstruction of harmful patterns in the mind.

Paul knew that we cannot resist evil unless we first cultivate an environment in our mind that can sustain the transformative paradigms of the Spirit.

Resistance begins in the mind as the Spirit cultivates an environment where the fruits of resistance can grow. Prophetic witness and leadership that resist oppressive structures, theologies, and ideologies flow from this source as our minds are renewed, our witness is empowered, and our communities are transformed through action.

Prayer: God of justice and hope, give me the courage to cultivate an environment in my mind where the fruits of your Spirit can grow and thrive. Transform me by the renewing of my mind, that I might resist evil in your name. Amen.

Rev. Colleen Hallagan Preuninger

*Aiah's daughter Rizpah took funeral clothing and spread it out
by herself on a rock. She stayed there from the beginning of the
harvest until the rains poured down on the bodies from the sky,
and she wouldn't let any birds of prey land on the bodies during
the day or let wild animals come at nighttime.*

—2 Samuel 21:10

R izpah's story is hidden, confused among the names of foreign kings and complicated lineages. But she is an icon of resistance. She resists the militaristic, death-dealing might of King David.

Rizpah was one of Saul's secondary wives. When David became king and began to consolidate power, he bargained with lives that were political liabilities for him—the lives of the sons of his old rival. But these were not just Saul's sons. They were Rizpah's too.

When David heard about Rizpah's actions to protect the bodies of her sons, blatantly resisting his authority, he was shamed into taking down the bodies and burying them with dignity.

Throughout history, the lives of the innocent are traded by people in power, and it is only the small but mighty actions of women like Rizpah that hold them to account.

Mamie Till Mobley was a woman like Rizpah. She resisted the pull of silence that allows sin to reign. She left her son Emmett's casket open after white supremacists brutally murdered him. When magazines printed the pictures of his mutilated body, US Americans were forced to confront the horrors of racism.

Neither Rizpah's nor Mamie's actions put an end to militarism and racism. But these women refused to be silenced and showed those in power a terrible truth. These women resisted, even though they felt like they had nothing—certainly nothing compared to the power of a king or Jim Crow. But their resistance was enough.

And our resistance can be enough too. Perhaps you, like me, are overwhelmed by the injustice in the world, wondering how small actions of resistance can actually make a difference. Perhaps you, like Rizpah and Mamie, are filled with grief and rage and don't care if you make a difference but will speak out anyway. They spoke the truth, naming the wrong that had been done to them. We can too.

What wrongs have you endured? Whom in power do you need to call to account? What truth do you have to speak?

Prayer: Mothering God, this world is so far from what you hoped for it. But you call me to live into that hope, to name the truth that the world should be, and to call out injustice. Give me the strength of women like Rizpah and Mamie to resist the Davids and Jim Crows of this world. Amen.

Rev. Shannon E. Sullivan

{Abigail} told her servants, "Go on ahead of me; I'll be right behind you." But she didn't tell her husband Nabal.

—1 Samuel 25:19

Like most women of the Bible, Abigail doesn't get a lot of space. Also like most women in the Bible, she earns every word she gets. She not only saves her home and livelihood, but she also keeps David and his men from committing atrocities. And, she does it all without permission.

David is on the run from King Saul and asks for some food from a farm owner named Nabal after protecting his shepherds and flock. After Nabal refuses, David decides it's time to pillage Nabal's home. As David's men advance, Abigail, Nabal's wife, runs out to meet David with food for his band of soldiers. Through her generosity, she saved everyone in her household. Abigail risked her life by going behind her husband's back. She risked having to live the rest of her life under his scorn. She risked being beaten by him or thrown out. She took the risk of disobedience because she knew the risk of obedience was worse. She knew that by doing nothing, she and everyone she loved would die. She knew innocent lives were at stake.

There are times in all of our lives when we decide we don't need permission, when lives hang in the balance and the "man in charge" doesn't seem to get the gravity of his decisions. For me, these times have ranged from starting new worship services to reaching new people to protesting white supremacists. Why would I risk my job and even my physical well-being? Because lives are at stake.

God comes, like the shepherds came to Abigail, and says, "You must do something or there will be death." In these moments, God's permission is the only permission we need. When we choose to resist the status quo and listen to God, we become daughters of Abigail. Let us risk our own comfort that others may live. Let us never choose to follow when those decisions mean destruction. Instead, let us protect life and prevent violence. Let us lead the resistance that changes the story.

Prayer: God, help me hear your voice loudest. When I am told to keep silent or to do what is wrong, help me resist like Abigail. In so doing, let me be an agent of peace. Amen.

Rev. Crystal Jacobson

⌒ A Prayer for Boldness ⌒

Righteous God, I feel you nudging me, no, pushing me to stand up for justice in this world. I know you call me to resist evil, injustice, and oppression. This feeling is overwhelming.

I want to do what is right. I want to do what is needed. I want to follow your lead.

So I pray for boldness. Give me not only the strength to speak and the words to say but also the spirit of power so that I might deliver your message in a way that changes things, changes the world.

Help me be bold. Take the quiver from my voice and the tremors from my hands.
Help me be bold. Pour into my heart a feeling of peace.
Help me be bold. As I take a deep breath to do what is right, help me be bold. Amen.

Rev. Sarah A. Slack

A righteous person giving in to the wicked is like a contaminated spring or a polluted fountain.

—Proverbs 25:26

In an arid environment like Israel-Palestine, a spring would have been a critical, life-sustaining resource. A community blessed with a fountain would have taken care to tend and protect it. Drought and erosion can temporarily or permanently kill a spring, but a contaminated or polluted spring means something else entirely. Pollution reveals a precious water source is being taken for granted. It reveals that people were unwilling or unable to put in the effort to protect life itself.

All too often, our world suffers ongoing injustice because of our own failure to step up and do the work.

For years, when I witnessed baptisms in my United Methodist Church, I heard the vow to "reject the evil powers of this world," but I missed the follow up "to resist evil, injustice, and oppression, in whatever forms they present themselves."[2] As an adult, it seems so clear to me now that rejecting evil is not the same as resisting evil. Rejecting is impersonal. It's passive. It allows us to stay comfortable over here while theoretically opposing the evil that is over there. But resisting requires that we come face to face with evil, to name what it is doing and the people it is hurting. It is hard and scary and risky to resist. It is much safer to reject an idea than to resist the actions that idea generates.

Clearly the writer of Proverbs was familiar with otherwise righteous people who would give way before the wicked. A contaminated spring gives no relief. It is a silent symbol of where hope could have existed, if only people had put in the effort. Likewise, a Christian who fails to resist brings no relief from injustice and is a reminder that staying silent only gives the upper hand to the wicked.

Prayer: Holy God, through the water of baptism, you have given us the freedom and power we need to resist all that is opposed to your beloved community. May

I never take for granted your life-giving grace and love. Give me this day the courage to use that power to bring relief and hope, for myself and for the needs of others. Forgive me for the times I have failed to tend to your springs of life, and give me the strength to continue in this sacred work. Amen.

Rev. Sharon L. S. Cook

*Speak out on behalf of the voiceless, and for the rights of all who
are vulnerable. Speak out in order to judge with righteousness
and to defend the needy and the poor.*

—*Proverbs 31:8-9*

I first came across these verses while I was volunteering in Venezuela
after college. Reading a modern Spanish translation (Dios Habla Hoy),
I loved the phrasing, "lift up your voice for those who have no voice." As I
translated materials and urgent action requests for a human rights advocacy
organization and a disaster relief collaborative, I took pride in using my
gifts, skills, and privilege as an English-speaking North American to draw
attention to the needs of those who had no "voice" in the public sphere
beyond their own communities.

Years later, I encountered novelist Arundhati Roy's response to being
called a "voice for the voiceless" through her writing: "There's really no
such thing as the 'voiceless.' There are only the deliberately silenced, or the
preferably unheard."[3] I realized I had unconsciously bought into the idea
that because I was advocating for justice, it was OK to substitute my voice
for the voices of those I was trying to help.

Having been encouraged in college and seminary to see myself as a
leader, and trained to step in and speak up when I see oppression and injustice, I now try to discern when my desire to help others is actually an
expression of privilege, bound up with classism or white supremacy. I have
started reading and following more thought leaders who are people of color
and continue educating myself to better understand the depth and breadth
of the "-isms" entrenched in our society and in my own heart and mind.

I still believe those in positions of authority must, at times, speak out,
defend the vulnerable, and do justice for those who are materially poor. But
this can begin with amplifying the voices of the "deliberately silenced" and
the "preferably unheard."

In my own life, I am working on stepping back to ask, "How can I contribute my time and resources to support the empowerment and leadership of those who have not had the advantages I have had?"

The work of resisting evil and oppression is not always flashy and feel-good, but we must trust that God is with us in the difficult, internal, complex, and long-term efforts too.

Prayer: God of self-giving love, you showed us in Jesus Christ that the first is to become last, and the last is to become first. Show me where the work of resisting injustice begins with my own attitudes, so that I may more faithfully embody your dream of right relationships for all people. Amen.

Rev. Kerry L. Greenhill

I'm convinced that nothing can separate us from God's love in Christ Jesus our Lord: not death or life, not angels or rules, not present things or future things, not power or height or depth or, or any other thing that is created.

—*Romans 8:38-39*

So many people try to tell us who we are. And who we aren't. You are not thin enough. You are too thin. You are too loud. You are bossy. You are abrasive. You are strong. You are too strong. Research has shown that as girls grow up, they become quieter and more compliant because the messages they receive consistently are that if they don't tone themselves down they are just too much.[4] We are just too much.

There are all kinds of people and pressures telling us who we are and where our value comes from. But here's the thing: what really defines us isn't those voices, but rather the love of God in Jesus Christ. God loves you—the real you—the you who isn't too much but is instead exactly enough. And there is nothing that can separate you from the love of God. Nothing.

Living a life of resistance means resisting anything that tries to separate you from your true identity as one who is deeply loved by God. Paul, the writer of this letter to the Roman Christians, believed strongly that there are forces at work in this world that are opposing God's own forces of Love and Grace. He called those powers Sin and Death. He writes these verses in Romans to encourage the early Christians by declaring that Sin and Death hold no sway over God. The power of God is greater than any other power. Unlike the powers of Sin and Death or the power that comes from positions of authority, elected or ecclesial or corporate, the power of God is not corruptible. God's power was made manifest in Jesus Christ who conquered Sin on the cross. God's power empowers us to show up as the person we were created to be: loved by God and living a life of radical love in the face of hate in this world.

Prayer: Loving Holy One who created me on purpose, put your strength in my heart as I resist the words of those who would have me be less than I am. Send your voice to my ears, so that I can hear your loving declarations louder than the words of anyone else. Empower me with your power, which is more just and loving than any power of this world. In your name I pray, amen.

Rev. Dr. Emily A. Peck-McClain

⌒ A Prayer in Times of Chaos ⌒

Make my heart and my feet be still, O Rock and Redeemer. The world around me continues in chaos—I cannot claim control over it. Instead, remind me of the breath of life that flows in me. In and out, in and out, in and out, continuously. O Rock and Redeemer, you are here. Within me. Around me. Always. Thank you. Amen.

Rev. Katie Black

⌒ A Prayer for the Gift of Life ⌒

Holy God, I am not always satisfied with who I am. I look in the mirror and don't like the reflection. I am not as thoughtful or witty as I wish to be. I am not fierce or strong.

But you gave me this life. And so, loving God, thank you. Thank you for this body, with its bumps and cracks and frizz that carries me day by day. Thank you for my mind as it thinks, contemplates, wonders, and wanders. Thank you for my heart as it breaks for your children and this world.

Help me see the beauty of this creation, this life of mine. Thank you for this life. Amen.

Rev. Sarah A. Slack

*Queen Esther answered, "If I please the king, and if the king
wishes, give me my life—that's my wish—and the lives of my
people too. That's my desire. We have been sold—I and my people—to be wiped out, killed, and destroyed."*

—*Esther 7:3-4a*

In her acceptance speech for the 2018 Golden Globe Cecil B. DeMille
Award for lifetime achievement, Oprah Winfrey said, "What I know for
sure is that speaking your truth is the most powerful tool we all have."[5]

Indeed, our most powerful form of resistance is showing up and unapologetically being our fullest, truest selves in the face of powers that would
silence us, enslave us, and destroy us.

Queen Esther shows us how it's done. Not without fear. Not without a
tribe. Not without a second try. But in the most basic and terrifying act of
living her truth for all the world to see. When the Persian king needed a
new wife, he rounded up all the eligible bachelorettes in the country and
ended up giving the rose to Esther. Esther was an orphan who was raised
by her older cousin Mordechai. They were Jews exiled in Persia. Now
that Esther was queen, Mordecai kept his relationship to her a secret. He
thought it was best no one knew she was a Jew, and of course, he would
end up being right.

The king's right-hand man, Haman, developed a grudge against
Mordechai, but rather than throw him in jail, Haman went full-on mani-
acal and decided to have the entire Jewish population in Persia wiped out.
Mordechai sent word to Esther that she needed to do something and quick.
So even though it was illegal, she requested an audience with the king.
Emboldened by the prayers and fasting of her fellow Jews, she was able to
reveal her truth, halting the nationwide assault on her people. When we
show up just as God created us to be (femme, butch, quiet, loud, taking up
as much space as we take up, loving the people we were born to love), when

163

we live as our true selves, we express the truth of our Creator. Truth always frightens evil. That's resistance!

Esther teaches us how to save the world:

1. Show up.
2. Be unapologetically yourself.

Not on the list: apologizing, staying silent, and trying to be some version of yourself the world is comfortable with.

Indeed, as long as injustice exists, we commit to making those with power uncomfortable.

Prayer: God of truth, help me reveal your nature by being exactly who you made me to be. Strengthen me in the discomforting work of being myself and resisting the evils that seek to change me. Amen.

Rev. Corey Tarreto Turnpenny

*In the depths of who I am I rejoice in God my savior. He has
looked with favor on the low status of his servant. Look! From
now on, everyone will consider me highly favored.*

—*Luke 1:47-48*

The act of birth—whether it be to a human being, to a church, or to a vision—is a radical act of resistance, hope, and believing there is still beauty waiting to be created in this world even in the midst of heartbreak and pain. Mary's Magnificat is an awe-inspiring example of this.

In the Magnificat, Mary reacts with hopeful anticipation to learning that, out of the depths of her being, a child will be born who "will rule over Jacob's house forever" (Luke 1:33). All of us are invited to participate by bringing love into the world.

The words of Mary's Magnificat gave me great power and refuge as I carried my second child, Riley. I struggled with the world as it was, what I believed it could be, and how I was called to resist. I struggled with how to explain the current state of our world to my new, mesmerizing baby alongside my inquisitive and engaged five-year-old. I struggled with how to do what we needed to do to ensure that our family and our communities were standing together and celebrating the magnificence and diversity of all of our neighbors.

In the midst of a time of uncertainty and fear, Mary's Magnificat and this new child were reminders to hold on to hope. They were reminders that together we could create a new world. I had all I needed within my resilient, remarkable, and powerful female body. I continue to hold onto the radical belief that the kin-dom of God is on its way and that I am called to be a part of creating it here on earth. How can I not be hopeful, staring at a beautiful child, who knows only love and peace?

What is it within you that is calling to be birthed? What are the deepest pieces of you that God is calling together to be a reminder of hope?

Prayer: Birthing God, train my eye to find power in the divine acts of resistance that I am required to be a part of as I seek to heal the communities of which we are a part. Tune my ear to hear what it is you are trying to radically birth from within me. Amen.

Rev. Laura Ann Gilbert Rossbert

What then shall I tell you, my Lady, of the secrets of nature that I have learned while cooking? I observe that an egg becomes solid and cooks in butter or oil, and on the contrary that it dissolves in sugar syrup. . . . what can we women know, save philosophies of the kitchen? . . . One can philosophize quite well while preparing supper. I often say, when I make these little observations, "Had Aristotle cooked, he would have written a great deal more."[6]

—Sor Juana Inés de la Cruz

Sor Juana Inés de la Cruz (1651–95) was a Mexican scholar, nun, and prolific writer who lived in an era that was not ready for her intellect, feistiness, or feminism. Her biting critique of the hypocrisy of men, the patriarchal norms of her society, and the church's perpetuation of sexism earned her condemnation by the Archbishop of Mexico City and other church leaders.

Nevertheless, she continued to advocate for the rights of women to study, even as those in power sought to silence her voice, confiscate her vast library, and censure her writing.

Responding to the Bishop of Puebla's argument against the education of women and his specific criticism of her, Sor Juana wrote a lengthy, precise, and brilliantly sarcastic response. Instead of simply arguing that a woman's place was not only in the kitchen, she turned this gender norm on its head by arguing, tongue in cheek, that a woman's time in the kitchen was an intellectual advantage that could have benefited Aristotle.

Sor Juana's will to fight, to survive, and even to thrive in a nunnery in seventeenth century colonial Mexico inspires those of us still facing ridicule, obstacles, or suppression by those same patriarchal structures over three centuries later. Resisting the people and systems that would silence her, she used sarcasm and wit to subvert her accusers' understanding of women and the God who made them in God's image.

Sarcasm continues to be a necessary tool of self-care amidst the resistance! Eventually forced to abandon her studies by her superiors, Sor Juana sold all of her possessions (by some counts, her books were confiscated), gave the proceeds to the poor, and dedicated the rest of her life to caring for the poor and sick. For all the ways the people and systems of the church had harmed her, Sor Juana's God-given intellect and faithful compassion could not be taken from her.

Prayer: God of faithful resistance, strengthen girls and women who are still fighting for education, a voice, and recognition of the gifts you gave us. May we all resist those who would silence us with such faithfulness as your daughter Sor Juana. Amen.

Rev. Angela M. Flanagan

A Prayer of Blessing to Be Who You Are

May you know you are worthy.

May you unlearn all the silence and shame you were taught through hints and insinuations.

May you stand tall and walk proudly, delighting in the shape and movement of your body as you travel through the world, spirit-in-flesh, breath-and-dust, beloved child and Imago Dei.[7]

May the truth woven into your being find its way out in words and music, in dance and poetry, in loving and marching, in creating and tearing down.

May you know your own power to speak and to listen, to make room for others and to claim what is yours.

May you be heard.

May you be seen.

May you take up space in the world.

May you know you are whole and holy, blessed and beautiful, bold and brave.

Be who you are: it is enough.

Amen.

Rev. Kerry L. Greenhill

*"How long will you act like a drunk? Sober up!" Eli told
her. "No sir!" Hannah replied. "I'm just a very sad woman. I
haven't had any wine or beer but have been pouring out my heart
to the LORD. Don't think your servant is some good-for-nothing
woman."*

—1 Samuel 1:14-16a

Others dismissed Hannah for much of her adult life. Dismissed her as
barren, a woman unable to birth children in a society in which fertility defined a woman's worth. Dismissed her as a complainer in a marriage
where her husband thought her life should be fulfilling enough. Eventually
Hannah went to the temple, where her sorrow poured forth from her eyes
and mouth, and she was filled with such passion that Eli, the priest, the
powerful, dismissed her once again. "Go home, woman," he said. "You're
drunk."

But this time, fed up with being put out, Hannah stood up. "No sir!"
Hannah said. "I am a woman of faith, and my sorrow, my passion, my life
is valid to God. Do not dismiss me. I will not be ignored."

Many of us have known Hannah's experience. We have been told to stop
worrying about things we think are important; been called scattered when
we lead with excitement and passion; been declared angry when we insist
on being heard. We can also know the rest of Hannah's experience.

We, too, can stand up.

When Hannah stood up, her world changed. Eli saw her for the woman
she was: broken, hurting, and deeply loved. Finally, she was seen.

Resisting oppression looks like knowing, despite others' voices, who
you are and that your experiences are valid. It means demanding to be
seen—and even more, known—as a person deserving of respect. You are a
child of God. You deserve to be known the way God knows you. You can
stand up. And more than anything else, you are loved.

Prayer: God who loves me beyond all understanding, you formed me in your image and declared me "beloved." May I live as if I know it. Give me the courage to stand up so that others may know it too. I pray this in the name of Jesus, the one who stood up for all of us. Amen.

Rev. Allie Scott

Our deepest fear is not that we are inadequate. Our deepest fear is that we are powerful beyond measure. It is our light, not our darkness that most frightens us.[8]

—*Marianne Williamson*

I walked out of the subway station in New York City and into a mass of people who were carrying signs and wearing pink hats. I was carrying a sign reading "Love Trumps Hate." I felt my palms getting sweaty. I followed the crowds into an area lined with barricades where thousands of people had marched ahead of me at the 2017 Women's March. I thought about the women throughout history on whose shoulders I stood as I marched through the streets of New York City, praying, chanting, and desiring change.

I thought about my own personal fear, watching our country become more divided through the 2016 election and wondering if we would ever truly stand united. I knew I would have work to do, but could one person really, truly be able to make a difference? Would I be able to resist injustice? Would I be able to stand up for my oppressed brothers and sisters? Would I refuse to let hatred dominate our world?

Marianne Williamson's words remind us that it's not about whether or not we are adequate enough; it's about whether we believe in ourselves. It's about whether we see how bright our light shines. God implores us to resist injustice. God beckons us to stand up for some and to stand up against others. God inspires us to resist hatred. God doesn't just request and require us to act; God also empowers us to do so through the Light. God gives us the Light, Jesus, who also reminds us to use that light we have from being baptized into him. And the Spirit comes alongside us when we do.

We must use our light to resist the hatred and darkness of our world. We must use our light to shine brightness into the places that remain in the shadows in our world. It can be frightening to condemn hatred, to take that first step marching for justice, and to speak our own truths. When we use our light, we are resisting the evil forces of this world and sharing with the world a new way: a way of love and light.

Prayer: God of justice, you empower me with your light to speak to the world of your kingdom come here on earth. Give me courage to accept that light and shine it into the world to bring more life, light, and healing to our broken world. Amen.

Rev. Kaleigh Corbett

Shadrach, Meshach, and Abednego answered King Nebuchad-nezzar: "We don't need to answer your question. If our God—the one we serve—is able to rescue us from the furnace of flaming fire and from your power, Your Majesty, then let him rescue us. But if he doesn't, know this for certain, Your Majesty: we will never serve your gods or worship the gold statue you've set up."

—Daniel 3:16-18

Bu ut even if he doesn't, we will never serve your gods."

This piece of this story continues to ring in my heart long after I read it. Often, this story is told primarily as a testament to the power of faith: God will rescue you in every circumstance if you just believe hard enough.

But I see it as an incredible story of resistance: the belief that the very act of standing firm in who God calls you to be is sacred, dangerous, and the ultimate act of worship.

When I was teaching at the United Nations with the United Methodist Women about the impact of mining on indigenous women, I heard someone tell the story of Sister Valsa John of India. She often spoke out about the mining sites that were encroaching on her village. She knew they represented lost resources and environmental devastation. She led the movement to resist the destruction of her land. She was killed for it. She refused to bow to the god of consumption, not because she knew God would protect her from harm, but because bowing before that idol was blasphemous to our Creator. She resisted, just as Shadrach, Meshach, and Abednego did, knowing that nothing is worth serving Nebuchadnezzar.

We are not created to be a people of resistance because it will be easy. We are not charged to stand up because we believe faith will shield us from consequences. We stand up to golden gods because we love God too much not to. We stand up to Nebuchadnezzar to save others from the furnace. We also stand together, just like Shadrach, Meshach, and Abednego, because there is strength in knowing you are not alone. Social movements are often rooted in faith communities because we recognize communal resistance as our sacred task.

May we continue to find courage in the strength that surrounds us, the faith that calls us into hard places, and the God who never abandons us.

Prayer: Loving God, grant me the strength to face the furnace and hold firm in my conviction. Grant me the wisdom to know when I should not kneel. Grant me the compassion to stand beside others as they resist the idols of destruction. I give thanks for your steadfast love that surrounds me always. Amen.

Rev. Janessa Chastain

⌒ A Prayer for a Social Justice March ⌒

Disquieting Spirit, you have stirred me from the depths of my heart to the soles of my feet, and so I march.

Christ, who loves this world enough to have walked its dusty roads on frail human feet, I take to the streets in your name, and so I march.

Holy Creator God, it is your vision of a healed and new creation that I seek to build with your guidance, and so I march.

I know this is but one way to join with my siblings, your beloved children, to be seen, heard, and counted. I pray that your arms enfold each marcher to keep us safe. I pray that your Spirit infuse the words we speak, the witness we give, and the signs we carry.

Make our resistance a holy one. Our hope is in you; renew our strength for your kin-dom's work. May we run and not grow weary, may we walk and not faint.[9]

And may this march not be the end, but only the beginning of what we can do for this cause. Amen.

Rev. Dr. Emily A. Peck-McClain

The daughters of Zelophehad . . . came forward. . . . "Why
should our father's name be taken away from his clan because he
didn't have a son? Give us property among our father's brothers."

—*Numbers 27:1a, 4*

Mahlah. Noah. Hoglah. Milcah. Tirzah. These five women resisted, and God was with them. As the Israelites were preparing to enter the Promised Land, their leaders were allotting land to all of the families, but these women faced a great injustice. Because their father, Zelophehad, had died in the desert and left behind only daughters—who, under current law, couldn't inherit property—they would be left out!

Without land of their own, this "Promised Land" would be a land of poverty and struggle. So what did they do? They decided to speak up as a united front for justice and challenge the status quo. Mahlah, Noah, Hoglah, Milcah, and Tirzah stood before Moses and all the people to name the injustice and demand an inheritance of land—a just, but unheard-of, request.

Here's the best part of the story. After hearing these women's grievances and their controversial demand, Moses resists his own knee-jerk reaction. He doesn't fall back on legal precedent or succumb to public pressure— both of which would have surely perpetuated this injustice. Instead, he recognizes that something bigger is afoot, and he turns to God for wisdom. And God responds! God says, "Zelophehad's daughters are right in what they are saying" (Numbers 27:7a). God sides with these sisters and affirms their right to inherit land. Going even further, God tells Moses that these women have set the legal standard from here on out! Because of their willingness to speak truth to power, not only is their own future in the Promised Land secured, but new policy is enacted for the Israelite people as well, and justice is ensured for generations to come.

Resistance starts with truth-telling. When faced with unjust systems and policies, we must first be willing to speak the truth about these injustices.

What injustices do you need to resist? What truth is God calling you to speak? God is in the truth business, and even though resistance is never easy, God will be with us in this holy work.

Prayer: God of Truth, thank you for calling me into your kin-dom of justice. Thank you for these bold, assertive women who teach us about resisting and speaking up when life is unjust. Thank you for giving me the tools I need to speak truth, especially when doing so against systems of power and authority. Help me recognize the truth you're calling me to speak and give me the holy courage I need to live into that truth. Amen.

Rev. Mary R. W. Dicken

The Spirit of the Lord is upon me,
  because the Lord has anointed me.
He has sent me to preach good news to the poor,
  to proclaim release to the prisoners
  and recovery of sight to the blind,
  to liberate the oppressed,
  and to proclaim the year of the Lord's favor.

—*Luke 4:18-19*

We turn on the news, read the paper, look at Facebook, and we see images and hear sound bites of unbelievably horrific events. The world is overwhelmed by the spiritual forces of wickedness. We feel devastated, defeated.

Yet, in baptism, we have claimed we accept the freedom and power God gives us to resist evil, injustice, and oppression in whatever forms they present themselves. The reality of living into that claim is hard for many of us. We don't know where to begin. Our voices aren't strong, our influence isn't great. What can we possibly do to make a difference?

According to the Gospel of Luke, when Jesus began his ministry he quoted the prophet Isaiah and then he went out to heal the sick, one at a time. His ministry didn't start with feeding five thousand people. He started by casting demons out from one man. Then he healed Simon's mother-in-law. Jesus began his ministry offering healing and hope to individuals.

We don't have to begin with some big feat that will change the world. We can start, as Jesus did, with one. We can support one cause with our time and our money to help bring good news to the poor. We can stand up for one person who is experiencing injustice and oppression. Once we take the first step, we will begin to see more ways in which we can resist evil, injustice, and oppression. We will begin to see people who will help us live out our vows. Our voices will become stronger. We will become bolder.

Prayer: Ever-present God, give me insight as to where to begin. Grant me courage and wisdom. Help me be bold so that I can live into my baptismal promise to follow Jesus by resisting evil, injustice, and oppression in all forms.[10] *Amen.*

Rev. Sarah A. Slack

Look! I'm doing a new thing;
*   now it sprouts up; don't you recognize it?*
I'm making a way in the desert,
*   paths in the wilderness.*

—Isaiah 43:19

Have you ever pondered a garden in the middle of winter? My partner is a gardener and prefers to grow vegetables he can cook for us to eat. In the winter, I can look at the garden patch, brown and wilted, and see flattened leaves where squash once grew or the last rotten grape tomato. What I don't see is any sign of life. Or any sign there could be life there again. But, my partner sees the rows of tiny sprouts he will tend and nurture once the weather turns warm until our table overflows with good food that tastes like sunshine. I know that feeling, too: the hope of seeing what's not yet there.

Seeing what God is doing in the midst of the reality of our lives, even when it seems like we're surrounded by circumstances of "not yet," is hope. This hope is an act of resistance.

We struggled with infertility for several years. We had an adoption fall through after we spent several days in the hospital with a sweet baby. We waited, anxious, measured in our hope during the process of IVF and the birth of our first child. We pondered and prayed as we waited to see how we might grow our family until we adopted two more children. But, in all of that time looking at the ground that wasn't growing anything, I could see our life as parents.

Even as we spent a year without weekly worship, our small crowd of faithful people dreamed for a new church. While caring for an old building we inherited that flooded regularly, I could see it. I could look at the empty sanctuary and see where a thriving church that welcomes all people—really welcomes them—would be, filled with life and people of all ages.

And now it's real. People greet one another in the lobby while reaching for the creamer or butter for their biscuits. They spill out of the lobby onto the front steps, chatting and meeting new neighbors as children run between their legs and hug friends.

It's a gift from God to see what isn't yet there. And it's an act of resistance. To look out at the wilderness of the world, the oppression and pain, the brokenness and injustice, the abuse and silence forced on people, and to be able to see what God is doing to bring hope and love, to raise up the outcast, to lift high the songs, cries, and demands of the voiceless. That is resistance. Look around you. Imagine. Listen. See the possibility. Resist the limitations of what is there and work for what could be, what will be in the fullness of God's love.

Prayer: God of all creation, open my eyes today to see what's not there . . . yet. Amen.

Rev. Anjie Peek Woodworth

∼ A Prayer at a Time of Violence ∼

After another act of violence . . . another mass shooting . . . another case of police brutality . . . another high-profile rape case . . . we feel numb. It is the same story. Calloused killers and abusers are protected by the same people in power who always protect them, while bereft families look the same, unconsoled in the streets. We don't have the energy to wail and lament anymore.

But, truth-telling God, you call us to weep anyway. And not just to weep, but to get on the phones and out in the streets in anger, serving the survivors with compassion, breaking the silence that protects those in power and perpetuates cycles of violence. Do not comfort us. Inspire us to resist apathy and insist on your peace and wholeness in our homes, our communities, and our world, always. Amen.

Rev. Shannon E. Sullivan

"Make up your minds not to prepare your defense in advance. I'll give you words and wisdom that none of your opponents will be able to counter or contradict."

—*Luke 21:14-15*

Y ou're not the one on trial," the victim advocate reminded me. "Just remember to breathe." I nodded. Big breath in. God, would speaking my truth be enough?

As the #MeToo movement stirred up the nation, I went to trial to witness against the man who had sexually assaulted me. Twenty months earlier, at the time of the assault, I had been alone. There were no witnesses. There was no national resistance to sexual harassment and abuse. In shock, I had barely managed to whisper my own resistance. But, each time I shared my story with my spouse, my best friends, my colleagues, and finally, the police, my voice grew stronger.

The week before Advent, I got up on the witness stand. I trusted Jesus that the truth would be revealed. All I could do was unveil my own authentic self. Every unveiling is an "apocalypse." In fact, the Greek word for apocalypse means just that: it is the revelation of what has been hidden. As I joined my voice with the cries of other victims and survivors, was I shaking? Or was the world shaking?

Powerful forces rightly tremble when they are revealed. People who benefit under old systems are terrified when those systems are revealed. Those worlds will collapse. It will be an apocalyptic shattering. This is Christ's promise: the coming end will not go unnoticed.

With each assault, someone's world as they know it ends. These endings are unseen, unbelieved, unrecognized, unheard. On the other side of trauma, the world feels different. In this new world, survivors reintegrate and re-create wholeness. God is in this new world, too, revealing a new identity and new strength—and God's judgment brings hope. In this new world, the God of Love is also the Lord of Hosts, the Word of Solidarity, and the Spirit of Truth. Jesus is both victim and survivor.

Look for the apocalypse. You'll know it by the terror and the truth. Me too.

Prayer: Spirit of Truth, breathe into me, so I can breathe with trust. Speak in me, so I can speak out boldly. Stir in me, so I can stir up justice. Holy Wisdom, Holy Word. Amen.

Rev. Diane M. Kenaston

If I said, "The darkness will definitely hide me; the light will become night around me," even then the darkness isn't too dark for you! Nighttime would shine bright as day, because darkness is the same as light to you!

—*Psalm 139:11-12*

I did not know exactly what I was going to say when I walked into the sanctuary to confront the people who had made the church an unsafe place for the love of my life. I was angry and I was afraid. This was darkness, night, and fear taking over where there should have been light.

We didn't know why. We had our guesses: Perhaps it was because I, their new pastor, am a woman. Perhaps it was our age. Perhaps it was because we were not the previous leaders. Perhaps we did not say the right things. Perhaps . . . Perhaps . . . Perhaps. . . . In the end, though, I knew what this hostility toward my husband was about. Just five years ago, this church had told me, "You are single and therefore do not belong." And now, I heard, "You have chosen a partner who does not fit in with us, so you still do not belong." All around me, the church had turned into a place of night.

Resistance seems impossible when your spirit is broken. When that happens, bullies seem bigger and you can't imagine standing up to them. All you know is that the night hates day because it means its end. Resistance is bright as day.

The psalmist was practicing resistance in this verse. There is a deep trust that day will break open the night, that the night doesn't hold the same power as before. That night is the same as day. This happens when truth is revealed and breaks open hardened hearts. Women can practice resistance by being present in the spaces where they are unwelcome and unexpected. Showing up means others are sometimes uncomfortable and try to maintain their power and control. They are keepers of the night.

Resisting means bringing the anger to light. Resisting means the hateful words are not hidden or protected anymore. Resistance means systems and habits are challenged instead of taken for granted. Resistance is not easy work. But, oh my, does God ever love resistance! Resisting the night calls forth daybreak.

Prayer: Dear God, shine your light into my fear of resisting. Empower me to bring that light to others even when I hear night trying to close in on me. Speak into my heart the freedom that comes with working toward day. Amen.

Rev. Emily L. Stirewalt

*But let justice roll down like waters, and righteousness like an
ever-flowing stream.*

—*Amos 5:24*

In the film *Roots*, as a slave ship traverses the Atlantic, the captain feels some obvious misgivings about the treatment of the Africans aboard. In one scene, the captain is in his quarters praying. The officer in charge of the slaves below enters. The captain, somewhat meekly, voices his concern over the treatment of the slaves as well as the conundrum he finds himself in as a Christian man. The officer replies, "Captain Sir, if I was you, with all respect, I'd leave Christ's Gospel for private prayer and meditation, and, oh, Sunday meetings of course." The captain, resigned, nods his head and goes back about his business.[11]

The church becomes ineffective when we are convinced that the gospel is private and should be compartmentalized behind closed doors, while not affecting the behavior of believers or actions of the church.

Injustice still flourishes today, even if we like to think it is not as obvious as a slave ship. Inequality is all around us and so, too, is a narrative counter to the good news of Christ. It's much easier to ignore the problems when we pretend we don't see them. The captain was only faced with the reality of the slaves when they were occasionally brought on deck for fresh air or to be sprayed down. Other than those few times, these irritants of his conscience remained chained in the dark below, out of sight, in an attempt to stay out of mind.

Are there issues we like to stash below deck so we can ignore them? Do we remain somewhat unbothered in our daily lives, oblivious to certain structural sins, until the stench of mistreatment happens to waft our direction? Perhaps even more disturbing that if the answer to either of the questions above is yes, then is not our faith creating a false dichotomy between spirituality and social justice? Private prayers, devotions, Sunday school, and Sunday worship become a mode of escapism for some, a retreat into a comfort zone, void of conflict and battered consciences.

The gospel confronts the world with a new vision of God's desire for creation. The good news presents us with a choice: Do we simply sail along with injustice in the belly of our ships, or do we go below deck, confront the results of our greed and sinfulness, release the shackles, and participate in God's vision for freedom of all humanity?

Prayer: Lord of justice and righteousness, bring me face to face with what I would rather keep hidden. Show me the shackles to unbind and the chains to break so that I may work with you to bring forth new life and hope where there instead has been death and despair. Amen.

Nicole de Castrique Jones

After eight days his disciples were again in a house and Thomas was with them. Even though the doors were locked, Jesus entered and stood among them. He said, "Peace be with you." Then he said to Thomas, "Put your finger here. Look at my hands. Put your hand into my side. No more disbelief. Believe!" Thomas responded to Jesus, "My Lord and my God!"

—John 20:26-28

While the disciples exult over Jesus's return, Thomas appears to doubt. He has not seen Jesus, and recent events have given him every reason to be wary. "I won't believe until I've seen the wounds," he says. The cross of Christ is the ultimate act of resistance, the center of the gospel; for this disciple, only the scars of that resistance will convince him that Jesus has overcome death.

So, Jesus shows up alive while looking like . . . death. What if Jesus had instead appeared in a glorified body, hair and skin just so, without any marks of his torture and crucifixion? It would be hard, in that case, for Thomas, or anyone, to believe that he was the same person or that he had traveled through death to return. It could very well have undermined the entire gospel message. Instead, Jesus showed his wounds and invites his friends to see and to touch—and Thomas believes.

Resistance is not pretty. And the resurrected life is not smooth and polished. Rather, as Rev. Asher O'Callaghan puts it, "maybe even resurrected life has some grit to it."[12]

When we resist oppression, discrimination, and the powers of evil and marginalization, we, too, are going to be wounded. Some of our wounds will be internal, but others will be manifest in our bodies. Rather than letting fear of being wounded keep us from resisting, or hiding the wounds we receive from those around us, let us move faithfully into the fray. Let us share our wounds, as Jesus shared his with Thomas. They are not weakness but strength, signs of fidelity and hope, and signals to others to carry on the fight.

Prayer: Resilient God, let me be unafraid to be wounded in my resistance and unashamed to acknowledge and honor those wounds. Through the challenges of standing up and speaking out, let Christ's broken body and unbroken promise be a guiding light and an example for me. Pour out your blessing on all my acts of resistance, that they might recall for others your resistance through the cross. Amen.

Rev. Shannon V. Trenton

You cannot, you cannot use someone else's fire. You can only use your own. And in order to do that, you must first be willing to believe that you have it.[13]

—*Audre Lorde*

We come from women who breathed hell's fire as they survived the bowels of slave ships, plantations, cotton fields, and dark Mississippi streets lined with Jim Crow polls. We come from women who birthed fire by giving life to generations of women who would become entrepreneurs, astronauts, community organizers, teachers, doctors, lawyers, entertainers, and preachers. We are women of fire.

As young children, we are taught to stay away from fire and rightly so. Fire can be dangerous if not properly handled and watched. Yet, fire is natural and necessary, one of the four Western elements of nature. We cannot exist without fire. However, if we are never taught the proper ways of handling fire, we live in fear of it, especially the fire within.

So why do we doubt our fire?

We doubt and hide our fire because fire spreads and can set ablaze anything in our way. We doubt our fire because it purifies and exposes. We doubt our fire because we are afraid of the greatness and brilliance that lies within us. We are women of fire, on fire, walking through fire, and setting the world ablaze.

Prayer: Dear God, the Creator of earth, air, water, and fire. Thank you for the fire you have set ablaze within each of us. Help me own this fire and to shine my light. Help me walk in brilliance and spread your fire of love, justice, and mercy wherever I go. Amen.

Rev. Dr. Theresa S. Thames

Persistence

In Scripture, many of the stories of women are not heroic; theirs are survival stories, stories of women who persist in spite of danger and rejection, in spite of shame and expectations. Yes, God has called us, even in the midst of struggle. And yes, God gives us courage and strength to resist. But we know that sometimes we are just trying to survive, to keep putting one foot in front of the other, to persist.

Persistence is when we must continue in the direction of our faith and call, despite those who would have us quit or change direction. When we are told that we are too young or too feminine or too butch or too angry to lead, persistence pushes us to take charge anyway. When we are told, on the floor of the United States Senate, that we may not speak, persistence goads us to speak anyway. When we are rejected for jobs we are qualified for, overlooked for awards we deserve, or simply too tired to continue, persistence does not permit us to quit.

And even when we think we can no longer persist, God does. God continues to be faithful, continues to lure the good from our worst experiences, continues to call us as co-laborers. In the devotions that follow, you will find that persistent God calling you to persist as well. You will hear the stories of women who persisted in Scripture, in history, and today. You will see yourself in a line of persistent women and see how, over time, that persistence prevails, bit by bit, changing the face of the world just as the persistent dripping of water can change the face of rock.

May these devotions give you strength to keep persisting. And may you rest securely in the knowledge that even if you falter, God will keep persisting. And together, we can transform the unyielding rock of injustice and fear to make way for abundance, love, and peace.

In that city there was a widow who kept coming to him, asking,
"Give me justice in this case against my adversary." For a
while he refused but finally said to himself, "I don't fear God or
respect people, but I will give this widow justice because she keeps
bothering me."

—*Luke 18:3-5*

My toddler daughter and I have matching "Nevertheless, She Persist-ed" T-shirts.[1] I want my daughter to be inspired by the courage of Senator Elizabeth Warren, who shared the words of civil rights activist Coretta Scott King in spite of the attempts of white male colleagues to silence her. I hope she insists her voice be heard and then advocates on behalf of all women. I hope she will never give up the relentless pursuit of justice, like the widow in Luke's Gospel.

This widow won't stop pestering the unjust judge until he relents and grants her justice. Although this woman is poor, vulnerable, and oppressed, she refuses to give up, using any means necessary—persistence, complaining, insolence—to convince the powers that be to change. She reveals God's compassion for the most vulnerable and God's deep desire for us to persist in our prayers, protests, civil disobedience, and nonviolent resistance until the justice of God's kingdom comes on earth as it is in heaven.

If we take on the role of the oppressed widow, we are reminded that God has not forgotten about our cries for justice and freedom. If we are the judge who has benefited from privilege and systems of oppression, we can find freedom in setting others free. May "Nevertheless, She Persisted" not simply remain a hashtag or slogan, but a way of remembering the widow's courage at the heart of the gospel, which sets us free.

Prayer: Holy God, help me persist in prayer and protest until your peace and justice permeate every aspect of our lives, our communities, and our world. Amen.

Rev. Lisa Schubert Nowling

When they had crossed, Elijah said to Elisha, "What do you want me to do for you before I'm taken away from you?" Elisha said, "Let me have twice your spirit."

—2 Kings 2:9

Social media has created the illusion that we all should, and can, be Elijah-style prophets. We each have a microphone to yell at the corrupt power of our choosing, doing a furious dance of conflict and confrontation. It is easy to believe that if we choose the perfect turn of phrase, we will be able to transform the world into God's vision for us. And then we find ourselves burning out, giving up social media all together, and realizing that standing alone was never God's plan.

It is almost impossible to persist in world transformation if you are trying to do it alone. Transformation is slow, difficult work that requires bringing your community along with you. It asks you to walk alongside people with whom you disagree. Transformation, as modeled by Elisha, is work that doesn't always yield the flashy headlines that Elijah-style prophesying will, yet it is the work of God. It requires patience, vision, and a double-portion blessing.

This blessing allowed Elisha's work to endure hardships so his miracles could change lives, and so all those he brought along with him could know God's love.

Persistence is prophetic work.

We persist because the road is long but we know it's worth walking.

We persist because we see good breaking through.

We persist because, while moments of yelling into the social media void can feel good, we know transformative action requires so much more.

We persist and know in the moments when it feels overwhelming, we can call for a double-portion blessing of our own, and God's love will pour down with abundance.

We persist when we invite people into conversation and continue to stand boldly where we have been called.

Prayer: God of wind and fire, I ask for your blessing in this moment. I am tired, and complacency feels so easy. Mold me in the image of your persistent prophets. Remind me of the power of your love to transform the world. Hold me in hope. Amen.

Rev. Janessa Chastain

He continued, "What's a good image for God's kingdom? What parable can I use to explain it? Consider a mustard seed. When scattered on the ground, it's the smallest of all the seeds on the earth; but when it's planted, it grows and becomes the largest of all vegetable plants."

—Mark 4:30-32a

When I was a little girl, I learned about the parable of the mustard seed: a small, unassuming seed that, if tended properly, could grow into a nice pretty bush with birds and everything. I often saw myself in this parable. Even though I was small, I mattered. And eventually, I would be big and beautiful and complete. But only when I began gardening as an adult did I realize what it actually meant for the kingdom of God to be like a mustard seed.

Because mustard is invasive. It shoots up and spreads and takes over the space of other plants. It doesn't matter that you had planned to plant tomatoes in that section. If mustard gets there, it's going to grow. And once mustard gets in, it's near impossible to get out. You can try to pull it out, but another shoot will inevitably sprout up. It's edible whack-a-mole.

Jesus isn't talking about the kingdom of God being like a beautiful bush that has finally grown up. He's talking about mustard: this pervasive, persistent plant.

So I was right, as a little girl, to see myself in the parable of the mustard seed and to believe that I mattered, despite my size. But this parable is about more than size or achievement. It's about demanding to thrive, no matter what plans and structures present themselves. It's about love running rampant and wild, even when those in charge whine about broken rules and crossed boundaries. It's about refusing to be erased and holding on to hope, even in the midst of oppression.

Living faithfully in the world isn't always easy. There is always something or someone willing to tell you how to live, who to love, or what to do. And yet a life of faith is so much more than a set of rules. May you see the movement of God's kingdom here and now as it grows beyond the boundaries already drawn.

Prayer: Tenacious God, as I look through my life's experiences, I can see how relentlessly you have loved me through it all. I am so grateful for your love. May your love and your grace give me the courage to live like mustard: steadfastly, adamantly, and most important, faithfully. Lead me, Lord, whatever may come. Amen.

Rev. Allie Scott

⌒ A Prayer for Surviving ⌒

Holy God, you know all that I've experienced.

You know the pain in my heart and the difficulties I've faced.

You have wept with me.

You have comforted me.

You have been angry on my behalf.

In these moments, remind me of your love and your continued presence
in my life.

Strengthen me to speak for justice and grant me the courage to follow your
call.

God, you have journeyed with me, never leaving me alone.

In these moments, remind me that I am yours; strong, beautiful, and
beloved.

Guide me by your Spirit all the days of my life. Amen.

Rev. Lorrin M. Radzik

When the wine ran out, Jesus' mother said to him, "They don't have any wine." Jesus replied, "Woman, what does that have to do with me? My time hasn't come yet." His mother told the servants, "Do whatever he tells you."

—*John 2:3-5*

In 2009, I rode my bicycle 3,400 miles across the United States in an effort to raise money for Blood:Water Mission. I did my best to train for this trip, but the truth is, before we started, I had never ridden my bike in the mountains.

By the third day of our trip, this proved challenging. We faced a ride of eighty-seven miles entirely through mountains. The day was, in short, treacherous. By midday, I was exhausted and every muscle in my body hurt. I pushed on with everything I had. By the time we hit mile sixty, I told my riding partner I was tired and unsure I could keep going.

Her response? "No you're not! Shut up and keep pedaling!"

This was the last thing I expected from her, yet it was exactly what I needed. I stopped whining, saving my breath and energy. I still was not sure I could make it, so I secretly hoped our support vehicle would stop and rescue me. They did approach us around mile seventy-six, but much to my dismay, they simply waved and cheered: "You can do it!"

I was really frustrated. At least I was until I rode one more mile. In that moment, as I came around the curve to see the lush green crest of the mountain, I saw the most amazing sign I have ever seen: "Next 10 Miles, Steep Downhill."

Downhill! I made it!

On that day, I could imagine no greater answer to prayer. If I had quit at mile sixty or seventy-six like I'd wanted, my hard work would not have paid off. I would have missed the reward, wondering if the first sixty miles had even been worth it—and if I could make it the rest of the trip.

Often, our lives feel like mountains. We push and work and persist far beyond our own imagined capabilities. As we climb proverbial mountains, we can't quite tell if the next curve will take us to the glorious mountain-top or will simply wind around to another steep, unexpected incline. It's easy to want to give up. But like Jesus, we have to listen to the people who tell us to shut up and keep going.

Prayer: Holy and loving God, thank for your gift of persistence that helps me to press on, even when there seems to be no way. Help me trust in you and turn over my struggles to you, believing that you will help me make a way, even when there seems to be no way. In Jesus's name. Amen.

Rev. Jen Tyler

Then God opened her eyes and she saw a well of water.

—Genesis 21:19a NRSV

Hagar's relationship with the living God helps her persist through times of trouble, and she becomes the mother of a people. Hagar first meets God after she runs away from Abram and Sarai, the slaveholders who owned her and abused her. She runs to a spring of water in the wilderness, and God finds her there. Because God sees her and responds to her in the wilderness, she gives God a name that means "God who sees" (Genesis 16:13 NIV). God sees her real self and her capacity although others in her life do not.

Later, Hagar finds herself in the wilderness again, this time because she was kicked out of her house, and this time with a son who depends on her. When their water runs out, she cries out to God in anguish. This time God opens her eyes, and she sees a well of water.

In these stories, God sees Hagar even when the people around her do not see her, and God opens her eyes to see what she needs to see. So it is with us. God sees us as leaders, and God's intention is to open our eyes to see what we need to see. Our job is to keep going to the spring of water in the wilderness. It is to keep looking for the well even when it's not totally apparent where it is, in trust that God will open our eyes at the right moment.

In leadership, this movement of looking for and going to the well is essential. God desires to keep filling us with the living water that is Jesus Christ so that we have strength to persist through whatever wilderness we might encounter.

What is your well? Where is the place you go to be refreshed and sustained? Who are the people who help you find wells in the wilderness? How do you stay connected to the living water, Jesus Christ?

Prayer: God who sees, help me trust that you see my real self and capacity. Keep my eyes open for the well that quenches my thirst and reminds me of the rich spring of water deep within. Help me lead from that place. In the name of Jesus, the living water, I pray. Amen.

Rev. Alison VanBuskirk Philip

He replied, "You must love the Lord your God with all your heart, with all your being, and with all your mind. This is the first and greatest commandment. And the second is like it: You must love your neighbor as you love yourself."

—*Matthew 22:37-39*

I will never forget my first Sunday at one of the churches I served. I was in the receiving line in the back of the church, desperately trying to connect names with faces while also introducing myself, when one woman stopped to shake my hand and calmly said, "You will never be my pastor. It's just not biblical." I was the first woman to serve as the pastor of that church.

As time went on, I got to better know the woman who rejected me. She would throw down verses like a gauntlet. In those moments, all I could do was claim my calling. I knew in my heart this was both how I was called to serve and where I was called to be. I knew that trying to explain context to her wouldn't change her heart and mind; only love could do that.

So I loved her. I smiled at her and asked about how her family was doing. When her husband received a difficult diagnosis, I was the first person she called. We would continue to pray together for his health in the days and weeks of uncertainty to come.

Some days, persistence is simply showing up. It is loving people even when they act in ways that make it difficult. But we must also walk the fine line between loving others and loving ourselves. We must know how what is being said may be able to be conquered through prayer and love, but also which situations are so toxic that we need to leave. That is the difficult balance Jesus speaks of when he says that we are to love our neighbors as ourselves. For me, persistence is showing up Sunday after Sunday and claiming who I am—a pastor—no matter what others may say, until love wins.

Prayer: Lord, I thank you that even when others stand against me, you stand with me. Help me be firm in your love even when others doubt. Help me persistently be who you have made me to be. Amen.

Rev. Michelle R. Bodle

∽ A Prayer When Overwhelmed ∽

Merciful God, I am overwhelmed. I'm worn out. I can't do all the things that must be done. I am empty and I have nothing left to give.

Help me, God; please help me.

You are the one who brought light in the darkness and swept across the waters to bring order out of chaos. Do that here today, God.

Show me just the very next step forward. Send me someone to remind me I'm not alone. Show me one task I can handle or just the next step that is in front of me.

Help me remember that you love me because I am, not because of what I do. Be with me in this moment, God. I can't go on without you. Be with me here and now. Amen.

Rev. Anjie Peek Woodworth

*For if you remain silent at this time, relief and deliverance for
the Jews will arise from another place, but you and your father's
family will perish. And who knows but that you have come to
your royal position for such a time as this?*

—*Esther 4:14 (NIV)*

Being a leader requires good self-care. Part of my self-care includes
intentional relationships with female colleagues who are also "in it for
the long haul." When we gather for time together, we often end up discussing
what it means to persist—to stay the course and help our communities
engage in the incremental change necessary to bring about the kingdom of
God on earth as it is in heaven.

Esther's entire narrative captures the essence of persistence. She is a
woman who stepped out in faith and continued to lead and serve her people,
even when the outcome was not clear. In the same vein, we also remember
that the social change Christians seek—the leaning of communities
and cultures toward justice, compassion, and the bringing about of the
kingdom of God on earth—does not just suddenly happen. The hand of
the Divine has been present, is present, and will be present in the future.
We don't exactly know what "such a time as this" is. But we do know that
even if we can't see the entire picture, we as leaders are still called to persist
in our work and to participate in God's creation of a new heaven and a new
earth.

May we be lifted up by the reminder that change—especially social
change—takes time. Many invisible and visible voices whisper truth
behind closed doors as groups of people learn about new ways of being.
We don't know how our individual and collective service for the greater
good will become realized in future days, months, and years. We are simply
called to persist, to use our gifts and graces in ways that transform the
world in ways great and small. And sometimes our words, our service, our

presence, are used by the Divine in unexpected ways "for such a time as this."

Prayer: May Christ continue to transform me as I follow his call for compassion and justice, and may my community continue to be changed by individual and collective service in ways more glorious than I can ever imagine on my own. Amen.

Rev. April Casperson

*The Twelve were with him, along with some women who had
been healed of evil spirits and sicknesses. Among them were Mary
Magdalene (from whom seven demons had been thrown out),
Joanna (the wife of Herod's servant Chuza), Susanna, and
many others who provided for them out of their resources.*

—Luke 8:1b-3

Mary Magdalene is one my heroes. Her story has been twisted and misrepresented by the tradition, and yet she continues to emerge as a woman who rises above the limitations of femininity of her day.

When we first meet her in Luke, we find out that she has been healed and is now traveling with Jesus. She is identified by the city from which she comes, not by her father or husband. We can safely assume she is an independent woman—a woman who, for whatever reason, is living on her own and looking out for her own needs. We don't have any idea what has transpired to give her the freedom and privilege to make this choice, but given what we can gather about women in the first century, this was an unusual way of living. Perhaps it is her independence that led Pope Gregory to declare that Mary Magdalene was the same as the woman who washed Jesus's hair with her feet.[2]

That's the thing about living in ways outside of society's expectations: people (especially those in power) get confused, they aren't sure what to do with you, and oftentimes they will try to undermine you. This is, sadly, the way things still are in our world. When women do things "they aren't supposed to," be it politics, science, business, or ministry, we have to work at least twice as hard for the authority and respect others receive by virtue of their title, position, or privilege.

When these burdens weigh heavily, I turn to Mary Magdalene as an example. She continued to travel with Jesus, supporting him and learning from him, even in a society that wanted women to be submissive and obedient. Her relationship with Christ, her persistence, and her passion are what led her to rise early the day after the Sabbath long ago when she discovered the risen Christ and was the first to declare that neither death nor tarnished reputations have the final word.

Prayer: Living God, may I find strength in your presence when the burden is heavy. Help me see your guidance, that I may continue on my journey and find hope in your ability to overcome even death. Amen.

Rev. J. Paige Boyer

Be glad in the Lord always! Again I say, be glad!

—Philippians 4:4

When most photographers set out to capture an image, they are careful to choose the appropriate lens. The lens of any camera frames, brings clarity, and affects where the eye is drawn to focus in the composition of the photograph. As photographers use the lens of a camera, they depend on the lens to tell them exactly what to give their close attention to. Every hour of every day, they affect the way they see and are present to what's happening in the world.

I am connected in both my pastoral and personal life with a number of women and men who struggle to maintain a "lens" that will help them keep moving forward in life, regardless of the circumstances. I care for them while also battling my own internal struggles, leaning on the comfort that comes from relying on the "victim" lens, or feeling "stuck." Neither of these require much of us but continued complaint or scapegoating of our problems.

Often, I have to be reminded of other women who were able to maintain a lens of perseverance. I think of Anna Howard Shaw, a leader of the women's suffrage movement, a physician, and one of the first ordained female Methodist ministers in the United States. While she persisted to graduate from theological school in the late 1870s, she suffered extreme poverty during this period, living in an attic in Boston. She was often exhausted, cold, and hungry due to a lack of resources and an unrelenting workload. Shaw was denied when first applying for ordination, but eventually became ordained by the Methodist Protestant Church. In her struggles to follow God's desire for her life, she persisted. She fought against ridicule and unimaginable odds to become a sign of hope for many women around her who dreamed of expanded opportunities.

We are able to persist when our joy is not held hostage to life's circumstances. As Paul encouraged the Philippian church, Anna is famously attributed as proclaiming, "I wake up every morning with a great desire to live joyfully." It's not a manufactured joy to save face and get through the day. It is a joy-filled lens we actively choose to view our lives through because of the hope we have in Jesus Christ. It is a choice that is always available to us by the power of God.

What lens are you viewing your life from today?

Prayer: Lord, help me never surrender the agency I have when life gets me down. May I always remember that you are near—forever ready to comfort, challenge, and sometimes carry me through my next faithful step. Amen.

Rev. Katie McKay Simpson

A Prayer for Postpartum Mental Illness

God,

I am supposed to be feeling great joy, but the pain is consuming me.

I feel alone, abandoned, overwhelmed.

I don't know if I can pull out of this deep hole.

I have to keep going for this baby I just brought into the world, but God, I need help.

I feel like a prisoner trapped in this new body, this new life, this house.

I need to hear you tell me that it will get better.

I need you to whisper in my ear that I will feel joy again.

I want to feel joy now, the joy that is on all of the visitors' faces.

I just want to feel an ounce of that. I know I am blessed.

I am so grateful for this baby, but this black cloud over my head just won't lift.

Hold me, your beloved child, as I hold this beloved child.

Never let go. Give me the strength to make it through.

Day by day, hour by hour, give me hope. Help me feel your love, comfort, and joy.

Amen.

Rev. Julia Singleton

But Jacob stayed apart by himself, and a man wrestled with him until dawn broke. When the man saw that he couldn't defeat Jacob, he grabbed Jacob's thigh and tore a muscle in Jacob's thigh as he wrestled with him. The man said, "Let me go because the dawn is breaking." But Jacob said, "I won't let you go until you bless me."

—Genesis 32:24-26

Have you ever wondered how much longer you can do this? What-ever "this" is: leading while fighting racist ideologies, serving while caring for a sick child or parent, getting your work done while dealing with your own anxiety. My friend cross-stitched the mantra "Nevertheless, she persisted" for me to put where I can see it every day, but sometimes I wonder.[3] I wonder if I can be like Jacob, persisting in seeking a blessing in spite of the pain.

Now Jacob is not a biblical character I usually compare myself to. In fact, my struggle with infertility and miscarriage seems a long way from Jacob's struggle in the wake of the trickery on which he has built his life. And yet, this story of wrestling is the story I find myself in. Jacob is all alone with his fear and guilt, thinking that his luck has run out. He acts not out of hope, but desperation. Desperation for a blessing. Jacob's is a story that reminds me that even without the blessing of a baby, I know there is still a blessing in this journey for me. Not the blessing I want and not even the blessing that I need—because I need to be a mother. But it is another kind of blessing. The blessing of persistence. We all could use this blessing—from those of us struggling against the failure of their own bodies, like I am, to those struggling against the violence of poverty and abuse and the failures of the world that are so immense as to seem insur-mountable. We could all use this blessing if we are like Jacob, wondering if there can ever be a future for us in this place and this work.

Because such is the blessing of persistence: that even when we feel alone, even when all hope has failed, even when we can't move forward any longer and our bodies are pulled out of joint—even then, we can prevail.

Prayer: Wrestling God, you know when my heart is heavy and my strength wanes. Help me persist anyway, to not let go until I have seen the blessings, even in the midst of the struggles. For I am not alone, and I can prevail. Amen.

Rev. Shannon E. Sullivan

*So then let's also run the race that is laid out in front of us, since
we have such a great cloud of witnesses surrounding us. Let's
throw off any extra baggage, get rid of the sin that trips us up,
and fix our eyes on Jesus, faith's pioneer and perfecter.*

—Hebrews 12:1-2a

If you would have asked me ten years ago if I would be a runner, I would
have laughed. Today, however, it is not uncommon to see me and some
of my closest girlfriends out on the pavement, slogging through the miles.
The early mornings never get easier, but I do look forward to the faces of
my run-sisters. Few conditions keep us from meeting. I run for me: for my
health, for my sanity, for my prayer life. What supports me when I do not
feel like running, however, is the pack of running women that I have come
to know.

When a new woman joins us for a run, the standard pleasantries are
exchanged. "Are you training for a race?" Usually, she'll respond with a
tentative "my first 5k." She may not see our grins in the dark of the morning, but we all know that if she sticks with us, she'll be joining us in longer
distances with heartier goals before she knows it. We know that the support of this community will carry us further than we ever thought we could
go alone. That was the case for me.

I am training for my first marathon, and I know that the biggest challenges I'll face will come from within me. My mind will want to give up.
My legs will be tired. What I trust, however, is the support of the women
who have run marathons before. Their advice and encouragement make
chipping away at my doubts, reservations, and fears just a bit easier.

There are days when life is exciting and the conditions are ideal. There
are also days where everything in front of us seems daunting and everything we have hoped for feels out of reach. God's gift to us in the race of life
is the community that surrounds us now and those who have gone before.

Someday we will be the ones to do the encouraging! Discipleship makes us examine our biggest challenges, most of which come from within. It is the blessing of community, past and present, which encourages us to throw off our baggage and follow Jesus to incredible places.

Prayer: God, help me sense and rely upon the presence of your saints who uplift, encourage, and challenge me so that I may be transformed not by crossing the finish line but through the journey. Amen.

Rev. Anna Guillozet

Whatever you do, do it from the heart for the Lord and not for people.

—*Colossians 3:23*

Sometimes I just can't muster the strength to "measure my life in love."[4] I can measure it in expenses that pile up and laugh in the face of my tight budget. I can measure it in disappointments and frustrations. I can measure it in failures. I can measure it in pints of ice cream I've stress-eaten. I can measure it in grief. I know I should see my glass as half full; I often hear that this is a great perspective. But what if the glass has a crack in it? How could it possibly hold any liquid at all? In that case, I think half empty is actually doing pretty good.

Sometimes I can tell that others are impressed with my unending list of woes as well. They are the ones who say, "Wow! I don't know how you got through that!" They say it with admiration, I think. I am careful, though, to respond with truth rather than put it on as some badge of honor. The truth is that I make it through because I have to.

When the sun comes up and a new day breaks, we can greet it with excitement and expectation. We can leave our beds ready to take on the day. We can drink our coffee in gratitude for another day to live, work, and praise God.

Or, we can drag ourselves out of bed because that's what we do. We put one foot in front of the other because that's what feet do. So we walk on and refuse to go down in flames. One step and then another and then another. Refusing to give up, refusing to give in. That is persistence.

This verse from Colossians might seem an unlikely imperative when we think about our half empty (or potentially cracked) glasses. But the author of Colossians says "whatever we do," so that must include all those steps we take because what else are we going to do? If our hearts are tired but steadfastly continuing, it is with those tired hearts that we do what we do for God.

God doesn't reject us when all we have to bring is determination. God doesn't reject our hearts when they are exhausted or broken or frustrated. God receives them with grace, no matter what shape they are in.

Prayer: God who knows me intimately, whatever I do, I will do it with you and for you, bringing all of who I am into your presence and service. I know that you embrace and love me—not some perfect version of me, but the real me. I promise I will not stop; I will persist. With my tenacious heart I pray, Amen.

Rev. Dr. Emily A. Peck-McClain

⌒ A Prayer in the Midst of Waiting ⌒

Patient God, I come before you today in the midst of waiting. It is so hard to wait.

Teach me to be patient and remind me of your love. Grant me peace and comfort. Restore my hope and confirm your presence in my life, even in the midst of the waiting.

In the name of Jesus Christ, I pray. Amen.

Rev. Lorrin M. Radzik

⌒ A Prayer of Praise and Thanksgiving ⌒

Gracious God, all good gifts come from you, and for this gift, I give thanks. The time of difficulty has passed, and you have guided me to peace. Your Spirit of love is with me, and I rejoice in your faithfulness. Guide me, too, to be faithful with what I have been given and to forever sing your praises, not only in joyous times but also in times of trouble. Today, O Lord, I give thanks and praise to you for this good and wonderful gift, which surely came from you. Amen.

Rev. Jennifer Zeigler Medley

Abraham approached {the Lord} and said, "Will you really sweep away the innocent with the guilty? What if there are fifty innocent people in the city? Will you really sweep it away and not save the place for the sake of the fifty innocent people in it?

—Genesis 18:23-24

It is clear that Abraham and God had a close relationship; and yet, there is still a dramatic power differential at play. God, after all, is still God, the Almighty One, the one with the power. I imagine it would have been easier for Abraham not to argue with or challenge God, and yet surprisingly, he does. Abraham reaches out to God with humility and resolve, not just once, but six times. He persistently challenges God, asking if the whole city will really be destroyed even if there are fewer and fewer righteous ones.

When the plan ahead did not seem to match up to the character of God as Abraham knew it, Abraham called God to account. He could have easily shied away from confrontation with God. He could have ignored the voice within him that knew the heart of God to be gracious and just. He could have allowed the negative voices to take over (who was he to argue with the one true God?).

Through his persistence, Abraham firmly grounds himself in relationship with God.

While we may not run into challenges quite like Abraham's with God, we will all face conflicts, challenges, or confrontations that would be easier to walk away from or ignore. When you face that next challenge, the next task that is insurmountable, the next complaint that threatens your resolve . . . remember your calling. You may not be the one with the most power, but you stand in a position that only you can hold. Do not let your circumstances or those around you or even the voices within you hold you back from standing your ground, raising your voice, and claiming your role.

Prayer: Holy Spirit, move within me and around me. Empower me with boldness and resolve, that I might not back down from the task at hand to which you have called me.

Rev. Jen Anderson

I waited patiently for the LORD;
{God} inclined to me and heard my cry.
{The Lord} drew me up from the desolate pit,
out of the miry bog,
and set my feet upon a rock,
making my steps secure.

—Psalm 40:1-2 NRSV

The first verse of this psalm always used to bother me. "I waited patiently" seemed so passive, so unlike my own experiences of persistent prayer and wrestling with God. It doesn't bother me anymore. During one of the most challenging experiences in my life, stunned by a loved one's cancer diagnosis, I lived in that desolate pit. Unable to free myself from the miry bog alone, I spent many hours in prayer. I did research on appropriate treatments and I cried out desperately to God. I knew God alone could help.

God heard my prayer, making my feet secure on the shaky ground of what became our new normal. My church community supported me, serving as my rock and surrounding my family with prayers, casseroles, and flexibility until my steps were more secure.

This psalm was my lived experience. The original Hebrew of that word *patiently* that used to bother me so much says something like, "waiting, I waited." This waiting is active and persistent. It is intentional and vital. It is an invitation not to live idly as time passes us by, but to persist in active hope.

We, like the psalmist, are called to be active in our relationship with God as we are persistent in prayer. God will not abandon or forsake us, but continues to offer mercy and steadfast love.

Prayer: Gracious God, in our times of deepest need, shine a light on our situation. Make a way out of no way, providing us the ability to move forward. Help us to sing a new song of praise, for you are our God and we are your people, always and forever. Amen.

Rev. Megan Stowe

Those who stand firm during testing are blessed. They are tried and true. They will receive the life God has promised to those who love him as their reward.

—*James 1:12*

"Y ou're just a stupid little girl who doesn't know what she's doing!"

Those words came flying at me one afternoon at work. When I looked up, I found an older man who hadn't takeen the time to knock on my door or sit in the chairs in front of my desk. Instead, he towered over me, and then angrily stormed out before I could respond.

I knew exactly what he was upset about. For months, our leadership had been discussing next steps. We recently had made a difficult but faithful decision, and it didn't come without heartache or anger. My job was to continue doing my best to lead our organization through necessary, faithful changes.

Several years later, when I was at a different job, he called me and asked to meet for lunch. I hadn't seen or heard from him since that day he shouted at me. Reluctant and afraid, I agreed to meet him. When I did, he uttered the most sincere apology, with tears in his eyes. For me, it was a moment of redemption, full of God's promises.

When faced with adversity, we have the option of giving in or persisting. With the help of God, we can stand firm and take the next faithful step, rather than let others define our direction. We can listen to the call of God on our lives and free the Spirit to work through us.

In James 1:12, we are reminded that the fruit of our persistence is the promise of God: new life and redemption. Sometimes, redemption is immediate. Other times, it might be years in the making, coming in ways we least expect.

So, dear sister, when you face adversity, when someone calls you a "stupid little girl," when you are dismissed by others as you seek to fulfill God's call: Persist! Stand firm! And remember that God has promised redemption and new life.

Prayer: Fearless God, when I am afraid, help me persist. When I am unsteady, hold me in your loving embrace. Remind me of your promises of new life and redemption, and spur me on toward persistent action, in the name of Jesus Christ, our Lord, Amen.

Rev. Lorrin M. Radzik

Mrs. Which's voice was grave. "Wwhatt ddoo yyou unndderr
sstanndd?"
"That is has to be me. It can't be anyone else. . . . There isn't
anyone else." . . .
"Do you have the courage to go alone?" Mrs. Whatsit asked her.
Meg's voice was flat. "No. But it doesn't matter. . . . It's the only
thing to do."[5]

—Madeleine L'Engle

A Wrinkle in Time tells the story of Meg Murry, a girl at the beginning of adolescence, who is pulled into a rescue mission of universal importance by cosmic friends. It won the Newbery Medal in 1963 and has been one of my favorite books since the fifth grade.

The fantastical plot was almost too frightening for me as a kid, but what moved me was the character of Meg: brilliant yet shy, treated as an outsider, but loved fiercely and fiercely loving in return. I wanted to be brave like her.

At this point in the novel, It, a disembodied brain seeking control over all life, has nearly broken Meg. She is rescued from her suffering at the last minute and realizes her younger brother remains within It's power, and only she can return to face the danger and save him.

We may never find ourselves in the same situation as Meg, but her journey remains an inspiration.

Meg isn't confident she'll overcome the dangers before her. She's afraid. She doesn't want to go alone. But she's resolved.

Mrs. Whatsit asks if she has the courage. She is not asking Meg to act without fear. She is asking Meg to see what is at stake, and, even knowing the threat to self, choosing to do the necessary thing. Choosing to persist. Not passing the buck, not hoping senselessly for the best, but taking responsibility and action, sometimes for no reason other than the risk of failure, is too terrible to bear.

It must not overtake the universe. Meg summons her best gifts—brilliance and love—and she persists, she gets it done.

Women have been doing just that since the dawn of time. The need to muster our courage doesn't make an effort any less heroic or holy. May you remember to be courageous when the need arises to get it done.

Prayer: Jesus our Christ, help me be brave. Grant that I may choose to act in courage, not out of necessity, but out of love. Amen.

Rev. Bromleigh McCleneghan

For I can do everything through Christ, who gives me strength.

—*Philippians 4:13 NLT*

I'm tired.

I'm a single mom of two. I'm the cook, maid, referee, accountant, disaster relief person, nurse, and chauffeur. I try to channel Mary Poppins but usually end up sounding like Batman.

I'm a pastor too. I'm supposed to visit everyone, attend every meeting, preach an awesome sermon every Sunday, meet with the youth and encourage the young adults, and network in the community. I'm the leader of the church most of the time, depending on the situation and whom you ask and the phase of the moon. I'm supposed to be excellent at all of this, as well as being caring and spiritual. I'm never supposed to be bitter or angry, hurt or depressed, or political.

My life feels like a bad experiment in how long I can be all things to everyone, functioning without enough sleep, fueled only by Tic Tacs and Diet Coke.

When my kids complain about dinner or someone wants me to do more in less time or I hear I'm not volunteering enough at my kids' school, I remind myself of something Brené Brown said: "If you're not in the arena also getting your ass kicked, I'm not interested in your feedback."[6]

We don't have time for criticism from the balcony. We're in the arena where it's hard and brutal and we're making it work.

Every. Single. Day.

Paul would have appreciated Brené Brown's words too. He knew about life in the arena. He literally wrote these words from a dank, cold Roman prison cell. Already he had endured the pain of being an outcast, and yet he persisted. He had been beaten, and yet he persisted. He had witnessed the death of friends and was waiting upon his own imminent death, and yet he persisted.

He persevered in his faith and continued to preach the good news because he remained grounded in Jesus Christ. He didn't bear the trials alone but shared them with his friends and coworkers in God's kingdom through his letters. He drew strength from knowing that, as a member of Christ's Body, he could draw from a strength that was not his own and persevere through whatever was thrown at him in the arena, and even more, rejoice in the midst of it.

The same is true for us. We can do all things—all things!—through Christ who strengthens us. By his steadfast presence in our life, there is no amount of criticism, rejection, or pressure, from the cheap seats or otherwise, that we cannot overcome to make it through.

Prayer: Pour out your Holy Spirit upon me this day to continue onward no matter what challenges I may endure. Remind me to stay grounded in your Son, Jesus Christ, drawing from him strength to persevere. Amen.

Rev. Danyelle Trexler

We shall someday be heeded . . . everybody will think it was
always so, just exactly as many young people think that all the
privileges, all the freedom, all the enjoyments which woman now
possesses always were hers. They have no idea of how every single
inch of ground that she stands upon today has been gained by the
hard work of some little handful of women of the past.[7]

—Susan B. Anthony, 1894

It is through the persistence of women whose names we know and do not know that today we have the right to vote, work, preach, govern, sit around boardroom tables, and lead inside and outside of our homes and families. Today, we give thanks to God for those who have gone before us. We do not take lightly the sacrifices they have made, the scars that they still carry on their bodies and souls, and the path they have given us to march onward in faithful persistence. We hear their call to continue seeking true equality for women of all ages, races, nationalities, and creeds.

May we not give up when the road ahead seems treacherous. May we, too, work hard for our children to live in a world where people treat and respect one another as equals, regardless of gender expression or race or nationality. May we one day, with God's help, see one another as God sees us: as God's beloved.

Prayer: God of us all, I give thanks for all those who fought for the rights and privileges that seem guaranteed today. I remember and celebrate the lives of women who gave the ultimate sacrifice of their own lives for my rights. God of every nation and people, I pray for women and children around our world who do not have basic human rights this day. I pray we will not give up the fight to seek justice for all your children. God, in whose image we have been made, I pray for a day in which women will be treated and respected as equals. I pray for equal pay. I pray for the end of sexual harassment and violence. We pray for women to be seen as you see us: as your children, your beloved, made in your image. God of mercy and grace, may your will be done on earth as it is in heaven. Amen.

Emily Scales Sutton

∽ A Prayer for Beginning ∽ the Day Over

Gracious God,

The day has only just begun and already there have been angry words, tears, and frustration. He didn't take the garbage out. She wouldn't get dressed. I dropped a coffee mug. I yelled. They cried. I cried.

I do not want to send my babies to school with tear-stained faces. I do not want to go to work upset. I want to crawl back into bed, pull the covers over my head, and bury this day.

But the day has only just begun. Your light is breaking through the clouds. Your Holy Spirit fills my lungs with fresh breath.

Wipe away my tears and frustrations. Help me forgive and accept forgiveness. Grant me moments of joy. Let me begin again. Amen.

Rev. Sarah A. Slack

My loved brothers and sisters, you must stand firm, unshakable,
excelling in the work of the Lord as always, because you know
that your labor isn't going to be for nothing in the Lord.

—1 Corinthians 15:58

It was moments before the graveside service was to begin when the funeral home director pulled me aside and said, "Since we are outside and we have quite a crowd, you may want to speak up a bit. Try to project as much as you can." His professional demeanor took on a more paternalistic tone. He went on to share anecdotally how he was always having to project to be heard by his teenage daughters. I knew he meant well, but the parishioners who overheard the conversation had a good laugh knowing that "soft-spoken" is not how they would describe their pastor.

I get it. Sometimes people see a female and think *quiet, meek, unassuming.* But the voices of women have long had to proclaim louder and bolder, carving out the space to be heard in sometimes unwanted places.

When I first started out in ministry, I may have been a bit rattled by such a last-minute pep talk chock-full of unsolicited advice and assumptions about my ability to, well, do what I do. I mean, as a pastor, I kind of talk a lot. But that was then. And after years of surprising people with my not-so-meek-and-mild voice, I learned to take such low expectations in stride and simply do my thing. I needed to persist in the timeless proclamation of God's hope, redemption, and salvation.

The call of God seems mischievously indifferent not only to appearances but also to experience and even "giftedness." But in a shame-saturated culture moderated by opinionated comment threads, persistence is key.

Persist in staying more focused on God than on your own insecurity.

Persist in being faithful to God's call rather than in pleasing the critics.

Persist in the face of failure—not letting fear of failure paralyze you from taking courageous steps in the path God has set before you.

Persistence is asserting your voice in whatever God-given tone you have, not modulating the key to conform to anyone else's standards.

Persistence claims the space and shapes the narrative: a narrative of a persistent God who delights in disrupting the world's assumptions using persistently faithful people.

Prayer: Relentless God, you have never given up on pursuing the redemption of your people. Fan within me the flame of persistence to be about your work no matter what the obstacle. Keep me focused, keep me bold, keep me in your persistent love. Amen.

Nicole de Castrique Jones

*A Canaanite woman . . . came out and shouted, "Show me
mercy, Son of David. My daughter is suffering terribly from
demon possession." But he didn't respond to her at all. . . .
But she knelt before him and said, "Lord, help me." . . . Jesus
answered, "Woman, you have great faith. It will be just as you
wish."*

—Matthew 15:21–23a, 25, 28a

We don't know her name, but we know she persisted.

Picture this scene: Jesus is traveling with his disciples, and a woman runs up to him, shouting for help because her daughter isn't well. The harried disciples, clearly on a mission to get to their destination, implore Jesus to tell the women to go away. Shockingly, he does—albeit somewhat more diplomatically than that. Jesus tells the woman that he's here for the Jewish people, not for people like her. It's not personal. Helping her just doesn't fit the mission.

The woman doesn't give up. She gets on her knees and begs. Jesus dismisses her again, this time not quite so nicely. He makes a rude comment about not throwing bread that is meant for the children to the dogs. (In case it's not clear, the woman and her people are the "dogs" in this metaphor.)

Thinking quickly, the woman retorts, "But even the dogs eat the crumbs that fall off their masters' table" (Matthew 15:27). Whoa. Can you imagine talking back like that to Jesus?

In a shocking twist, Jesus affirms the woman for her faith, and her daughter is immediately healed.

In this story, a determined woman fights for what she knows is right. She refuses to take no for an answer and even has the audacity to turn Jesus's words back on him in an effort to change his mind. This woman demands that Jesus see her and her daughter as people worthy of his attention. She was told repeatedly to stop, but she nevertheless persisted.

Few people like conflict. When faced with pushback, our tendency is to quiet down and keep everyone happy. The cause of justice, however, requires persistence through awkward and uncomfortable confrontation. How is God calling you to persist in the fight for what is right? Commit to boldly persist, even when you're told to stop, and know that God is with you.

Prayer: Holy One, thank you for this persistent woman whose name is lost but whose story lives on. She reveals that persistence is a virtue. Give me the drive to press forward for the cause of justice even, and especially, when faced with resistance. Help me persist when I'm told to go away or when my concerns are dismissed as irrelevant. Remind me in those difficult moments that even Jesus needed to be challenged by persistent people of faith. Amen.

Rev. Mary R. W. Dicken

Notes

CALL

1. Jen Hatmaker, *Of Mess and Moxie: Wrangling Delight Out of This Wild and Glorious Life* (Nashville: Thomas Nelson, 2017), 100.

2. Jarena Lee, *Religious Experience and Journal of Mrs. Jarena Lee Giving an Account of Her Call to Preach the Gospel*, rev. and corrected (Philadelphia: self-published, 1849), 11.

3. Anne Lamott, Facebook, March 23, 2015, www.facebook.com/Anne Lamott/posts/654002261396087.

4. Mary A. Hanson, "What Was Martha Doing? Diakonia in Luke 10:38-42," Mary's Sword website, November 18, 2014, https://stromerhanson.blog spot.com/2014/11/what-was-martha-doing-diakonia-in-luke.html.

5. Rebekah Lyons, *Freefall to Fly: A Breathtaking Journey Toward a Life of Meaning* (Carol Stream, IL: Tyndale, 2013), 162.

6. Joann Wolski Conn, "Dancing in the Dark: Women's Spirituality and Ministry," in *Women's Spirituality: Resources for Christian Development*, ed. Joann Wolski Conn (Eugene, OR: Wipf & Stock, 2005), 27–28.

7. Mother Teresa, *No Greater Love*, ed. Becky Benenate and Joseph Durepos (New York: MJF Books, 2000), 148.

8. Elizabeth Gilbert, *Big Magic: Creative Living Beyond Fear* (New York: Riverhead, 2015), 238.

STRUGGLE

1. Psalm 139:1 (NRSV).

2. Luke 22:44.

3. Gloria Gaynor, vocalist, "I Will Survive," by Freddie Perren and Dino Fekaris, recorded October 23, 1978.

4. Catherine Keller, *On the Mystery: Discerning Divinity in Process* (Minneapolis: Fortress, 2008).

5. Julian of Norwich, *Revelations of Divine Love* (Blacksburg, VA: Wilder, 2011).

6. Paraphrase of Hosea 2:14 on the wall of Our Lady of the Desert Church, Tucson, Arizona.

COURAGE

1. Brené Brown, Facebook, February 14, 2018. www.facebook.com/brene brown/posts/1973287522686347.

2. Karen A. Waldron, Laura M. Labatt, and Janice H. Brazil, eds., *Risk, Courage, and Women: Contemporary Voices in Prose and Poetry* (Denton: University of North Texas Press, 2007), 22.

3. Rachel Held Evans, *Searching for Sunday: Loving, Leaving, and Finding the Church* (Nashville: Thomas Nelson, 2015), 188.

4. Brené Brown, *Rising Strong: How the Ability to Reset Transforms the Way We Live, Love, Parent, and Lead* (New York: Random House, 2017), 4.

5. Frances E. Willard, *A Wheel Within a Wheel: How I Learned to Ride the Bicycle with Some Reflections by the Way* (Bedford, MA.: Applewood, 1997), 20.

6. Willard, *Wheel Within a Wheel*, 16.

7. William H. McRaven, "Adm. McRaven Urges Graduates to Find Courage to Change the World" (YouTube). May 16, 2014, https://news.utexas.edu /2014/05/16/mcraven-urges-graduates-to-find-courage-to-change-the-world.

8. Hal Taussig, *A New New Testament: A Bible for the Twenty-first Century Combining Traditional and Newly Discovered Texts* (New York: Houghton Mifflin Harcourt, 2013), 226.

9. Taussig, *New New Testament*, 226.

10. Many phrases in this prayer are from Psalm 22 (NRSV).

RESISTANCE

1. Ada Maria Isasi-Diaz, a mujerista theologian, used the term *kin-dom* instead of *kingdom* when referring to the reign of God in her work "Kin-dom of God: A Mujerista Proposal." This term takes away the hierarchical and especially patriarchal nature of the word *kingdom* and uses a different term to emphasize the community and liberation.

2. "Renunciation of Sin and Profession of Faith," *The United Methodist Hymnal* (Nashville: The United Methodist Publishing House, 1989), 40.

3. Arundhati Roy, "Peace and the New Corporate Liberation Theology," lection presented at The 2004 Sydney Peace Prize lecture, November 3, 2004, Seymour Theatre Centre, University of Sydney, http://sydney.edu.au/news/84 .html?newsstoryid=279.

4. Dori Baker, *Girlfriend Theology* (Cleveland: Pilgrim, 2005), 1.

5. Oprah Winfrey, Golden Globes acceptance speech, quoted in the *New York Times*, "Read Oprah Winfrey's Golden Globes Speech," by Giovanni Russonello, January 7, 2018, www.nytimes.com/2018/01/07/movies/oprah -winfrey-golden-globes-speech-transcript.html.

6. Sor Juana Inés de la Cruz, *The Answer/La Respuesta: Including Sor Filotea's Letter and New Selected Poems*, trans. Electa Arenal and Amanda Powell, expanded edition (New York: Feminist Press at The City University of New York, 2009), 35.

7. *Imago Dei* is Latin for "image of God." You are made in the image of God.

8. Marianne Williamson, *A Return to Love* (New York: Harper Collins, 1992), 190.

9. Isaiah 40:31.

10. "The Baptismal Covenant I," *The United Methodist Hymnal* (Nashville: The United Methodist Publishing House, 1989), 40.

11. *Roots*, directed by David Greene (1977; Burbank, CA: Warner Home Video, 2007), DVD.

12. Asher O'Callaghan, keynote speech, Gay Christian Network 2018, Colorado Convention Center, Denver, January 19, 2018, www.youtube.com /watch?v=fsUM7ydXTDI, 2:30:21-24.

13. Rudolph P. Byrd, Johnnetta Betsch Cole, and Beverly Guy-Sheftall, eds., *I Am Your Sister: Collected and Unpublished Writings of Audre Lorde*, Transgressing Boundaries: Studies in Black Politics and Black Communities (New York: Oxford University Press, 2011), 3.

PERSISTENCE

1. Amy B. Wang, "'Nevertheless, She Persisted' Becomes New Battle Cry after McConnell Silences Elizabeth Warren," *Washington Post*, February 8, 2017, www.washingtonpost.com/news/the-fix/wp/2017/02/08/nevertheless-she

-persisted-becomes-new-battle-cry-after-mcconnell-silences-elizabeth-warren /?utm_term=.90c1a8a75835.

2. Heidi Schlumpf, "Who Framed Mary Magdalene?" USCatholic.org, The Claretian Missionaries, April 2, 2016, www.uscatholic.org/articles/200806 /who-framed-mary-magdalene-27585.

3. Wang, "Nevertheless, She Persisted."

4. "Seasons of Love," written by Jonathan Larson, in *Rent* (Broadway musical), January 25, 1996.

5. Madeleine L'Engle, *A Wrinkle in Time* (New York: Farrar, Straus, and Giroux, 1990), 216, 218.

6. Brené Brown, "Why Your Critics Aren't the Ones Who Count" (video), 2013, 99U Conference, November 6, 2013, 00:08:51, https://vimeo. com/78769611.

7. Susan B. Anthony and Ida Husted Harper, eds., *The History of Woman Suffrage*, vol. 4, 1883–1900 (Indianapolis: Hollenbeck, 1902), 223.